SPIRIT, SOUL & BODY

by

ANDREW WOMMACK

Spirit, Soul & Body
ISBN 1-59548-063-3

Copyright © 2005 by Andrew Wommack Ministries, Inc.
850 Elkton Dr.
Colorado Springs, CO 80907

Published by Andrew Wommack Ministries, Inc.

TABLE OF CONTENTS

Introduction

On March 23, 1968, I had a supernatural encounter with the Lord that revolutionized my entire life. For the next four and a half months, God's love completely overwhelmed me both day and night! Tasting God's presence in such a profound way ruined me for ordinary life. My expectations of my relationship with the Lord and my hopes of what He'd do through me literally shot through the roof. As far as I was concerned, Jesus could do anything!

However, once the emotion of it finally subsided, I felt worse than ever before. My inner expectations and my everyday experience remained worlds apart! The spiritual realities I knew in my heart just weren't manifesting themselves in the physical realm any longer. I longed to experience God again in that same way.

During this period of time, I was drafted and sent to Vietnam. Over there, temptations abounded! Many times I was the only Christian I knew. Everyone else gave themselves to the drugs, alcohol, and prostitutes that were so readily available. Even the bunker where I lived was papered with pornographic images— walls, ceiling, everywhere! Although this constant pressure to sin seemed unbearable at times, I refused to give in.

Out of sheer desperation, I started seeking the Lord by praying and studying the Bible as much as sixteen hours a day! This gnawing inner frustration motivated my quest to discover *"how I could get from here to where I knew in my heart I could be."* I knew Vietnam would change me, so I figured it might as well be for the good!

God began renewing my mind through His Word. Then I started experiencing that same divine reality as before—only this time it wasn't just in a physical, emotional way. The Lord revealed truths that changed my thinking and released His power in me. Joy and excitement came back again, but now they were based on understanding from the Word. I could recall Scripture and rejoice in it any time I wanted. In this way, God's Word began to produce an abiding stability in my life!

This understanding of spirit, soul, and body was one of the first revelations I received through studying the Bible. It not only alleviated the frustration and confusion I had but has served as a foundation for almost everything the Lord has shown me since. These important truths freed me from the bondage of much wrong thinking and enabled me to consistently experience God's supernatural power. Personally, I cannot comprehend how anyone can truly prosper in their relationship with God apart from understanding this basic revelation!

Today, I'm just as excited about this understanding of spirit, soul, and body as when God first showed it to me over thirty-five years ago. In fact, I've seen the Lord set more people free through this one teaching than almost anything else I've ever ministered! What you now hold in your hands has the potential to revolutionize your entire Christian life!

Chapter 1

God's Mirror

"**And the very God of peace sanctify you wholly; and I pray God your whole <u>spirit</u> and <u>soul</u> and <u>body</u> be preserved blameless unto the coming of our Lord Jesus Christ**" (1 Thess. 5:23, emphasis mine). Even though God's Word clearly teaches that we are three-part beings, very few Christians practice a functional understanding of spirit, soul, and body in their everyday lives!

Most people actually believe that they're only made up of body and soul. They confuse soul and spirit as being basically the same thing. Therefore, on a day-to-day level, they only acknowledge a physical part and an emotional, mental, inner part (commonly called "personality").

Even *Strong's Concordance* fails to distinguish all three! The Greek word for "spirit" is "pneuma" and is defined as being "the immortal soul." I don't mean to criticize anyone's work, but my study of God's Word has revealed a very distinct difference be-

1

tween spirit and soul. Therefore, I disagree with this particular definition of the word "pneuma." Your spirit is your innermost part, not your "immortal soul."

Your body is obvious. It's the physical part of you that can be seen in a mirror. If you were talking to me face to face, you'd be seeing my body.

However, you'd be speaking to my soul, which is my mental, emotional part. Some people define "soul" as being your "mind, will, and emotions." While that's certainly true, it's incomplete because your conscience should also be included. Your soul is what most people call their "personality."

No Natural Access

You can feel both your body and your soul. If I put my hand on your shoulder, you'd know that I touched you. However, I can also touch you whether I'm physically near or not. By speaking to your soul, I can make you glad, sad, or mad. Through my words, I could even "hurt" you without physically touching your body. It's easy to know how you feel in your body and soul because you're constantly in touch with them!

By taking a mental inventory, your body can instantly tell you how it feels. You know if your adrenaline's pumping or if you're tired, if you're healthy or fighting a cold, if your head aches, or if the shower's just right. In fact, you don't even really have to think about it because your body constantly feeds you such information.

You can also check your soul and know right away how you're doing. It's easy to tell if you're happy or hurt, mentally worn out or sharp and ready to go, or just plain angry. You'd even be aware of fear or depression if it came because you're always in touch with your soul.

However, your spirit cannot be accessed in any natural way. Jesus declared, **"That which is born of the flesh is flesh; and that which is born of the Spirit is spirit"** (John 3:6). He meant that there's no direct connection between the two. They are interrelated, as you'll later see, but spirit is spirit and flesh is flesh. You simply cannot contact your spirit through your emotions or your physical body. Herein lies one of the great problems of the Christian life!

If you don't understand that spiritual reality can't be felt, then you'll be confused when God's Word declares that you have the same power that raised Jesus from the dead (Eph. 1:18-20). If you think truth can be discerned through your natural senses, then you'll be baffled when the Bible says that you're a brand-new creature who can do the same miraculous works that Jesus did (2 Cor. 5:17, John 14:12). Without understanding spirit, soul, and body, you'll search your body and soul in bewilderment wondering, *Where is it? I don't really have that kind of power in me. The Bible is so hard to understand!* If you can't see, taste, hear, smell, or touch what the Word reveals about you, you'll immediately be thrown into conflict. This apparent disparity between your experience and God's Word will cause you to throw up your hands in frustration and conclude, "It must not be true!"

Unlocking the Spirit Realm

Understanding spirit, soul, and body unlocks the spirit realm so you can experience who you are and what you have in Christ!

Since the spirit realm can't be naturally seen or felt, the only way to accurately perceive spiritual truth is through the Bible. Simply take God's Word and believe it!

Jesus said, **"It is the spirit that quickeneth; the flesh profiteth nothing: the words that I speak unto you, they are spirit, and they are life"** (John 6:63). God's Word reveals spiritual reality. If you want to know what your spirit is like, you must find out from the Word. You can't just go by emotion or some other type of perception. God's Word is spirit and life!

When you look into the Bible, you behold yourself in the spirit. **"For if any be a hearer of the word, and not a doer, he is like unto a man beholding his natural face in a glass: For he beholdeth himself, and goeth his way, and straightway forgetteth what manner of man he was. But whoso looketh into the perfect law of liberty** [God's Word, specifically the New Testament]**, and continueth therein, he being not a forgetful hearer, but a doer of the work, this man shall be blessed in his deed"** (James 1:23-25, brackets mine). God's Word is a spiritual mirror!

A Perfect Reflection

When you look at your face in a mirror, you aren't really seeing yourself. Rather, you're viewing a reflection. In fact, your eyes have never looked directly into your own face. Think about it—you've always seen a reflection! Even though it's only a representation, you've learned to trust it.

If you want to know if your hair is combed or if your makeup is on, you don't just go by how you feel. Since those things can't be felt, you must look in a mirror and then trust what you see. It's the same with your born-again spirit!

God's Word perfectly reflects who you are in the spirit. It's the only way you can know. You can't just assume, "If I had God's power inside of me, I'd be aware of it" because that which is Spirit is spirit and that which is flesh is flesh! It would be like trying to feel if your makeup was on or your hair was combed. Those things just can't be felt! You must look in God's mirror and trust the spiritual reality you see!

Confused

Every born-again believer has undergone a complete inner transformation. **"Therefore if any man be in Christ, he is a new creature: old things are passed away; behold, all things are become new. And all things are of God, who hath reconciled us to himself by Jesus Christ"** (2 Cor. 5:17-18). Notice how it doesn't say that "all things are becoming new" or "have the potential of being new." This verse declares **"old things have passed** (past tense) **away," "all things have become** (present tense—reality right now) **new,"** and **"all things are of God."**

If you don't understand spirit, soul, and body, you're instantly set up for confusion, frustration, and ultimately unbelief when you see a verse like this. After reading about a total change and all things being of God, you look at your body and immediately start wondering because it hasn't passed away or become brand new. If you were overweight before receiving the Lord, that didn't change the moment you got saved!

A time will come when you'll receive a glorified body, but that hasn't happened yet. **"For this corruptible must put on incorruption, and this mortal must put on immortality"** (1 Cor. 15:53). Although Christ's atonement provided for you physically, your body has not yet been saved. It's been purchased, but not yet redeemed.

S&H Green Stamps

As a kid, I collected S&H green stamps. Whenever my mother bought groceries, we would earn stamps according to the amount of the purchase. She gave them to me so I could keep them organized and paste them into a book. Then she'd take me to an S&H Green Stamp Redemption Center to turn in my completed books and choose anything I wanted of equal value from their store. Although the stamps were purchased, they weren't redeemed until I turned them in. It wasn't the stamps themselves I wanted but what I could redeem them for!

Jesus purchased your glorified body through His death, burial, and resurrection. Although full payment has been made, you still have a corrupted body while you wait to receive your immortal, incorruptible one. At this moment, you don't yet have the redemption of the purchased possession (Eph. 1:14).

Your soul wasn't saved either! This sounds strange to many people because they use terminology like *"I'm a soulwinner!"* and *"I came to see a soul saved"* to describe an evangelist and evangelism. In reality, the New Testament only mentions "soul salvation" a few times—and none of them, in context, are talking about the born-again experience (Heb. 10:39; James 1:21, 5:20; 1 Pet. 1:9). Soul salvation happens when an emotionally discouraged and mentally defeated Christian starts believing God's Word and then experiences victory, peace, and joy again. However, when it comes to being born again, your soul wasn't the part of you that completely changed!

If you were stupid before you were saved, you're still stupid after being saved. If you didn't know math before being born again, you won't instantly know math afterwards either. In fact, if you were depressed before you got saved, you'll stay depressed until you change the way your soul thinks by believing God's Word.

Your soul can be transformed now to the degree you renew your mind, change your attitudes, and conform your values to the Word of God. This should happen, and it's in the process of happening, but it didn't automatically happen. In your soul, old things didn't pass away, and all things haven't yet become new. The transformation of your soul won't be completed until you go to be with Jesus!

Where the Change Is Complete!

When you receive your glorified body, you'll also receive your glorified soul. First Corinthians 13:9-12 reveals how, when that which is perfect is come (your glorified body), your current partial knowledge will give way to full revelation. You won't know in part anymore, but you'll know all things even as also you are known. That's the coming future fulfillment of transformation and completed change in your body and soul!

But 2 Corinthians 5:17 clearly states that any person who is in Christ is *right now* a brand-new creature! Old things <u>have</u> <u>passed</u> away. All things <u>have</u> <u>become</u> new. This total transformation isn't just in process; it's describing a change that's already been done—an accomplished fact.

Where did this complete change occur? According to God's mirror—not in your body and not in your soul, but in your born-again spirit!

Chapter 2

Release What You've Already Got!

Your spirit totally changed at salvation! Upon making Jesus Christ your Lord, your spirit underwent an instant and complete transformation. Typically, your body and soul are both impacted by what happened, but it's not total, nor complete.

People who don't understand that the change took place in their spirits and has to work its way out into their souls and bodies are usually quite disappointed. "I thought I'd become a brand-new person. Jesus was going to change everything!" Then unbelief takes hold. "But things didn't change, and I'm still the same!" Some may seriously doubt whether or not they were saved. Those who do maintain their salvation often lose faith that they'll ever really experience and enjoy it here in this life.

But the truth is—your spirit has totally changed! You aren't in the process of trying to get anything from God. Everything you'll ever need in the Christian life is already present in its en-

9

tirety in your spirit! At this very moment, your born-again spirit is as perfect and complete as it'll ever be throughout all eternity. You won't get a new one when you arrive in heaven, and neither will it need to be matured, completed, or cleaned up from any defilement down here on earth. Your spirit is—right now—as perfect, mature, and complete as Jesus Himself!

The Pivot Point

After being born again, the rest of your Christian life consists simply of renewing and releasing! As you renew your mind and believe God's Word, your soul will agree with what's already transpired in your spirit. When your soul comes into alignment with what it sees in God's spiritual mirror, what's already in your spirit releases into your soul and body. That's how you experience the benefits of your salvation!

If your spirit and soul agree, you experience the life of God. Your born-again spirit is always for God because it's already been completely changed into His likeness and image. When your soul agrees with your spirit, that's two parts of your being against one. Since the majority always rules, your soul and body will experience the life, victory, and power that is in your spirit.

On the other hand, the supernatural flow of life from your spirit to the physical realm stops when your soul agrees with your body (majority rules again) and is dominated by the natural realm. You cut yourself off from experiencing God's life in you when you align your soul with what you can see, taste, hear, smell, and feel instead of what you perceive in the Word. What's in your spirit must flow through your soul in order to get out to your body and the physical world around it!

The Real You

Take a look at the functional diagrams I've included here. I call them "functional" because there's no inspiration or reality to the fact that I've depicted spirit, soul, and body as circles. None of us are circles, even though some people are rounder than others! These diagrams are just an effort to communicate with you the relationship between spirit, soul, and body by means of illustration.

Consider this first diagram of three circles inside each other (appears like a target). The outer circle is your body. It's the part you can see and feel. Then you have an inner part that can't be seen but can be felt. That's your soul. Notice how your soul touches both your body and spirit. Your spirit is a second inner part. Although it's the center of who you are, it can't be seen or felt.

Most people don't recognize the fact that their spirits are the core of their beings. They function primarily out of their soulish realm, believing what they think and feel is reality. They may perceive their souls to be the core of who they are, but God's Word says differently.

Your spirit is the real you! **"For as the body without the spirit is dead, so faith without works is dead also"** (James 2:26). After God formed Adam, He breathed into him the breath of life (Gen. 2:7). This Hebrew word "breath" is also rendered "spirit" in other places (e.g., Job 26:4 and Prov. 20:27). Adam's body and soul (physical, mental, and emotional parts) had no life in them until "spirit" was imparted. Your spirit is your life-giving part!

Since your life comes from your spirit, it's the innermost circle of the three. Notice also how your spirit is completely surrounded by your soul. It has no direct access to your physical body. The diagram of three rings also illustrates this lack of a direct link. That's why everything that comes out from your spirit to your body must go through your mental, emotional part!

Is Your Valve Open?

With the pipe diagram, one side represents your spirit and the other your body. Your soul acts as a valve in between the two. When you open the valve, what's in your spirit can flow through to your body. Depending upon how open it is, the flow of life could be just a trickle, a small stream, or rivers (John 7:38). When the valve is closed, the flow from spirit to body shuts off. That's a great illustration of how a born-again believer functions!

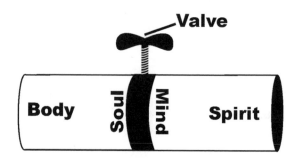

In your spirit, you've got the same power that raised Jesus Christ from the dead (Eph. 1:18-20). However, it's possible to have this power and never manifest it. If your soul, like a valve, stays closed to this truth, you won't experience it. Without opening the valve by renewing your mind to God's Word, the eternal reality in your spirit won't be able to impact the temporal "reality" of your physical realm. All that resurrection life and power just stays locked up inside until you look into the spiritual mirror long enough to see the real you and release it!

You could actually die with all of the power that raised Jesus from the dead sitting untapped within you. It would be like dying of thirst while leaning against a well full of life-giving water! If you're dominated by what you feel, your soul is agreeing with the natural realm. "I feel sick and my body hurts. The doctor said I'm dying. Here's my medical record to prove it!" Even though you have the resurrection life of God in your spirit, your soul can keep it shut off so that not one drop of life-giving power ever touches your physical body.

You can experience depression, anger, and bitterness all the while possessing God's love, joy, and peace in your spirit (Gal. 5:22). Since this applies to every area of your life, can you see how pivotal your soul is?

Your body doesn't really control anything. It just goes with the flow of what it sees, tastes, hears, smells, and feels unless otherwise influenced by the soul. It's amoral—neither good nor bad. Left to itself, your body just reacts to and goes along with what's happening in the physical realm.

When your soul agrees with your spirit, the life of God in you will manifest itself in your physical body. You'll experience healing, deliverance, anointing, victory, power, joy, prosperity— on and on it goes!

Victory Begins

Since most Christians don't have a working knowledge of spirit, soul, and body, they're dominated by what they can see, taste, hear, smell, and feel instead of God's Word. The flow of life within stays turned off because they don't believe anything they can't see. Neither do they understand the change that happened in their born-again spirits, nor are they fully aware of who they are in Christ. To them, something's just not real if it can't be perceived though their five natural senses. Attempting to be "honest," they search their physical, emotional, and mental realms for God's power. If they can't perceive it, then they must not have it.

However, the truth is that old things passed away, and all things became new in your spirit the moment you were born again. Now, everything you'll ever need in your Christian life is already there. Just renew your mind and release it!

This truth revolutionized my life! I had experienced God's power and reality, but when the emotion of it wore off, I thought they were gone. I knew God and everything He promised was real, but I thought I had to try to get Him to give me things. Due to my wrong thinking, I went through a period of discouragement, frustration, and desperation—not from sin but from a sincere desire to live for Him and experience His best. I felt like no matter how hard I tried, I could never get there. Then I started to see that God had already given me everything in my born-again spirit. As this revelation dawned on me, I realized that I just needed to release it. This simple understanding changed everything!

Since then, I've recognized that the Christian life isn't a process of "getting from God." Instead, it's a process of renewing my mind and learning to release what I've already received. It's much easier to release something I've already got than to go get something I don't yet have!

This erroneous concept of trying to get something you don't yet have carries within it an element of doubt. You see a promise in the Word concerning healing, joy, victory, power, provision, or whatever, and since you know God loves His children and keeps His promises, you start heading toward that, "believing God." You know it's possible—even promised—but since you can't perceive it yet in your mental, emotional, or physical realms, you don't believe it's already been done. In your mind, God's promise isn't a "reality" until you physically have it.

"I've Already Got It!"

My wife and I went through a period of extreme poverty when we were just starting out in full-time ministry. After coming home from Vietnam and getting married, I pastored a small church in Segoville, Texas. Every penny we had went toward paying the bills. We were so poor that sometimes we even went without food for a week or two!

During this time, my Bible kept falling apart. The pages had mildewed from Vietnam's humidity, and I'd written on them quite a bit. Despite my efforts to tape it together, entire chapters—even books—were gone. There I was pastoring a church with a beat-up, incomplete Bible!

Since we didn't have the money available to just go buy a new one, I decided to make an issue out of it. "How can I believe God to minister salvation, heal the sick, cast out devils, and change people's lives if I can't believe Him to supply me with enough extra money to purchase a Bible?" I drew my line in the sand and declared, "I'm going to win this fight or die trying!"

The devil took me up on it and the battle raged. Thoughts of fear and unbelief bombarded my mind. *Some man of God you are! You don't even have a whole Bible. You can't even believe*

God for a book! Some pastor you are—failure! I fought those thoughts constantly for six whole months!

Finally, I got the money and bought my new Bible. After having my name engraved on it, I victoriously paraded out of that bookstore carrying my trophy under my arm. All those negative thoughts left instantly. Once I had it, I never doubted that I'd get my Bible again!

"Of course not, Andrew, you already had it. Why would you doubt something you've already got?" My point exactly! God placed everything you'll ever need inside your born-again spirit. Once you believe you've already got it, doubt is eliminated!

You aren't trying to get saved, you were saved! You aren't in the process of being born again, you were born again! When you confessed Jesus Christ as your Lord and Savior, your spirit instantly changed. In your spirit, you are brand new and complete. God has already given you everything you need. The rest of your Christian life isn't learning how to get from Him but rather discovering how to release what He's already placed within!

Chapter 3

Renew, Acknowledge & Experience

Paul prayed for his friend **"that the communication of thy faith may become effectual by the acknowledging of every good thing which is in you in Christ Jesus"** (Philem. 1:6). "Communicate" means to "release" or "transfer." For instance, I'm communicating, releasing, transferring to you what God has spoken and made a reality in my life. "Effectual" means it begins to "work" or "produce." How does your faith work and produce? **"By the acknowledging of every good thing which is in you in Christ Jesus."**

Old Testament principles don't necessarily apply to New Testament faith. That's why concepts like "getting more faith," "receiving a new anointing," "getting more of God," and "receiving a double portion" don't work. Out of ignorance, people say, "Elisha had a double portion of Elijah's anointing. Tonight is double-portion night! Come up here and we'll pray for you to receive twice as much anointing." Elijah didn't have the fullness of God. He only had a small part. Therefore, Elisha could have twice as much as Elijah. However, John 1:16 reveals, **"And of his fulness have all we received, and grace for grace."** Under the New Covenant, we have all received (past tense) His fullness!

As a believer, God gave you everything when you were born again. Old things passed away, and all things became new. In your spirit, you received the same measure of faith, the same power, the same wisdom, and the same ability as every other Christian. Our spirits are all identical to the Lord Jesus Christ in every way. Your spirit isn't in the process of growing and maturing because it's already complete; you've already got everything!

The rest of your Christian life is learning how to manifest in the physical realm what's already in your born-again spirit. The way your faith becomes effective, productive, operative is by acknowledging every good thing in you (your spirit) in Christ. Since you can only acknowledge things that already exist, you can't acknowledge something that's not a reality. Therefore, in order for your faith to work, you must recognize, believe, and acknowledge the good things in you in Christ!

One-Third Complete

I didn't see any manifestation of power, victory, joy—anything—until I started renewing my mind and discovering what God had put inside me. As I began acknowledging what He had already done, His presence and power started manifesting in my life. The lives of the people I ministered to began to change. Acknowledging the good things in me in Christ caused my faith to work and produced supernatural results!

Most Christians believe God can do anything but experience very little. Now that they've been born again, they know they have access to the Lord. They believe that God can release

His power in answer to prayer, but whether something comes to pass or not depends on their performance (i.e., being holy, speaking right, studying the Word, tithing, avoiding strife, etc.). This view short-circuits God's power because their focus is on what they need to do instead of what Christ has already done. It's not His power these Christians doubt but rather His willingness to use it on their behalf. They think God's power is out there somewhere, and they must do things in order to obtain it!

The truth is, when you were born again, God put His power, anointing, victory, joy, peace—everything—in you in abundance. The only reason they aren't manifest in your soul and body is your unrenewed mind. It's not that God didn't give it but that you're still looking at the physical realm instead of His spiritual mirror.

One-third of your salvation is already complete! Right now, your spirit is as saved, sanctified, holy, and empowered as it will ever be throughout all eternity. Someday you'll receive a new body and a new soul to match up with your new spirit. Until then, it's your soul and body that are in the process of change, not your spirit. At the Second Coming of Christ, or when you die and go to Him, the change in your soul will be instantly completed. Then when the Lord returns, your spirit and soul will be reunited with your glorified body. At that time, all three will be perfect. But until then, the Christian life is renewing your mind and acknowledging the perfection already in your spirit so that your soul and physical body can experience the benefits of salvation!

Conformed or Transformed—It's Your Choice!

"I beseech you therefore, brethren, by the mercies of God, that ye present your bodies a living sacrifice, holy, acceptable unto God, which is your reasonable service. And be not con-

**formed to this world: but be ye transformed by the renewing of
your mind, that ye may prove what is that good, and acceptable,
and perfect, will of God" (Rom. 12:1-2).**

*Don't be conformed to this world! "Conformed" means "to
be poured into the mold of." In life, you will encounter pres-
sures—from the world, from the devil, from unbelievers, and from
circumstances. Although you can't avoid being melted, you can
choose which mold you'll be poured into. When pressure comes,
will you become bitter or better? As fiery trials arise, will you
stand victorious or give in to defeat? The choice is yours, but you
will be changed!*

Be transformed by the renewing of your mind! "Transformed" in the Greek is the same word we derive "metamorpho-
sis" from. It's the picture of a little worm spinning a cocoon and
then coming out as a butterfly. The way you transform, change,
metamorphose from being bitter, hurtful, sick, and defeated into
the loving, healed, healthy, and victorious person that God created you to be is through renewing your mind. Your spirit is already changed, and your body is basically your soul's caboose.
Whatever you think in your soul, your body will just go along for
the ride. Therefore, it's your mind, your thoughts, your attitudes
that determine whether you experience victory and the life of
God in your spirit or the defeat and death of the fallen natural
realm. Renewing your mind to the Word facilitates your transformation!

God's Word tells you what is spiritually true. It gives you
the new values and attitudes you should conform yourself to. As
you continually look into the Lord's spiritual mirror, you'll begin to see and experience yourself for who you really are!

Chapter 4

Reality—Carnal or Spiritual?

"For to be carnally minded is death; but to be spiritually minded is life and peace" (Rom. 8:6).

Carnal mindedness doesn't necessarily mean "sinful" mindedness. All sin is carnal, but not all carnality is sin. "Carnal" literally means "of the five senses," or "sensual." Carnal mindedness is allowing your mind to be dominated by what you can see, taste, hear, smell, and feel. You are carnally minded when your thoughts center primarily on the physical realm.

Even in the natural, you've learned to believe in things you can't see. Radio and television signals constantly surround you. Microwaves heat your food. Because of germs, you wash your hands, whether they look dirty or not. Although these physical things can't be seen, you're still very aware of their presence in your life.

However, there's also an entire spiritual world—including realities within you—that exists beyond your natural perception. Your brain and five senses can't perceive it, but your soul can through God's Word. By faith, you can believe things that can't physically be seen!

Let Peace Flow!

Spiritual mindedness releases the flow of God's life in you, but carnal mindedness shuts it off. Simply stated, carnal mindedness = death, and spiritual mindedness = life and peace (Rom. 8:6).

"Death" means "anything that's a result of sin." This isn't limited only to the ultimate physical death of your body but includes all of death's progressive effects as well (i.e., sadness, loneliness, bitterness, illness, anger, poverty, etc.). In this fallen world, being dominated by your natural senses produces death.

But spiritual mindedness produces life and peace! Jesus declared, **"The words that I speak unto you, they are spirit, and they are life"** (John 6:63). When your thoughts are dominated by what the Word says, you're spiritually minded.

It doesn't matter what your physical circumstances might be—God can keep you in perfect peace! **"Thou wilt keep him in perfect peace, whose mind is stayed on thee: because he trusteth in thee"** (Is. 26:3). As your mind stays on Him, your soul agrees with your spirit, and God's peace is released into your soul and body. Your born-again spirit is always in perfect peace—it's just a matter of drawing it out!

On the other hand, you won't experience the peace within when your mind stays fixed on your problems. Peace—an emotion—is linked to the way you think! Your lack of peace isn't because of any circumstance or person; it's just that you've allowed your mind to be dominated by what you can see, taste, hear, smell, and feel. You're busy thinking about the potential damage, considering what the problem has done to others, and hashing through their opinions on the subject. All the while, God's peace has been present in your spirit, but you haven't drawn it out. Open that closed valve and let peace flow!

Alienated Through Ignorance

Believers shouldn't live like lost people who are trapped in their carnal, physical world. **"This I say therefore, and testify in the Lord, that ye henceforth walk not as other Gentiles walk, in the vanity of their mind"** (Eph. 4:17). In context, "Gentile" was a non-Jew, someone not in covenant relationship with God. In other words, unbelievers don't use their minds to perceive spiritual truth.

Ephesians 4:18 talks about **"having the understanding darkened."** If you don't renew your mind and use it to study and meditate God's Word, it'll automatically gravitate toward what you can see, taste, hear, smell, and feel. This darkens your understanding.

Understanding is the application of knowledge. "Knowledge" puts food into your mouth and chews. "Understanding" actually swallows and digests it so that the beneficial nutrients can be released into your body.

The knowledge of God is critical, but must be understood to be useful. Without understanding, you can't release the life that's in it.

When a Christian walks like an unbeliever, they get the same results—death. Believers who don't understand and apply the knowledge of God in their lives gravitate toward carnal

23

mindedness. Without spiritual knowledge and understanding, your mind can't be renewed, and the life of God in your spirit can't be released. That's why understanding this revelation of spirit, soul, and body is the first step toward walking in life and peace!

When a believer's understanding is darkened, they are **"alienated from the life of God through the ignorance that is in them, because of the blindness of their heart"** (Eph. 4:18). In other words, the life of God is still there, but they are alienated from it due to ignorance, which refers to the mind. This is where most Christians live their lives—separated from the life of God within, due to their own ignorance of spiritual truth.

In His Word, God declares that by His stripes, you were healed (1 Pet. 2:24). You look at yourself and ask, "Is that cancerous tumor gone?" Still feeling pain, emotionally drained, and fearful, you continue, "God says I'm healed, but I'm not. It's still there, so I must not be healed." By adopting that attitude, you've allowed your five senses to dominate you more than God's Word. The same power that raised Jesus from the dead is in you, but you didn't believe it (Eph. 1:18-20). You let your mind be controlled by what it saw in the physical realm more than the spiritual realm. Therefore, even though you have the resurrection life of God in your spirit, it won't manifest in the physical realm because you're carnally minded, which equals death.

Engine or Caboose?

Lasciviousness = controlled by what you feel. **"Who being past feeling have given themselves over unto lasciviousness, to work all uncleanness with greediness"** (Eph. 4:19). There's a godly type of feeling. You don't just deny that your senses exist. However, most people have gone beyond simply receiving sensory input to being dominated by them. They've left what God intended feelings to be and entered into lasciviousness—where feelings run their lives.

Feelings should be the caboose not the engine. They were designed to follow what you think, not lead the way. When you let the caboose act like the engine in your life, you'll find yourself either going nowhere or heading straight for a train wreck! For a believer, this should not be!

The Spiritual Approach

"But ye have not so learned Christ; If so be that ye have heard him, and have been taught by him, as the truth is in Jesus: That ye put off concerning the former conversation the old man, which is corrupt according to the deceitful lusts; And be renewed in the spirit of your mind; And that ye put on the new man, which after God is created in righteousness and true holiness" (Eph. 4:20-24).

Renew your mind to the Word, and put on the new man! Ephesians 4:24 plainly reveals that your born-again spirit—the new man—was created after God in righteousness and true holiness. You need to recognize and acknowledge your true self in God's mirror. Right now in your spirit, you are righteous and holy!

At times, you might think, *I'm getting holier,* but in reality, you're just referring to your actions in the physical realm. The degree of holiness you live outwardly may vary, but the nature of your born-again spirit is righteousness and true holiness.

That's why you must worship Him in spirit and truth! **"God is a Spirit: and they that worship him must worship him in spirit and in truth"** (John 4:24). Your spirit is the part of you that completely changed. Old things passed away. All things became new. You cannot approach God unless you come to Him through the righteousness and true holiness of who you are in the spirit.

You aren't worthy to come into His presence based on the righteousness and holiness of your thoughts and actions. Even at your best, you still fall short of doing everything you should. Even when you've been seeking the Lord wholeheartedly, you still have negative and impure thoughts in your mind. No matter how hard you try, you'll never measure up to God's perfection through your own efforts in the physical, emotional, and mental realms.

How then does God in His holiness fellowship with you if even at your best, you still fall short of His standards? He communes with you Spirit to spirit! You became a brand-new creature who is now righteous and holy. In your born-again spirit, you're as pure as Christ is because His righteousness has been given to you. **"But of him are ye in Christ Jesus, who of God is made unto us...righteousness"** (1 Cor. 1:30). Jesus Himself literally became your righteousness!

From Rags to Righteousness!

It's inaccurate for a New Testament believer to confess "All of my righteousness is as filthy rags!" (Is. 64:6). You either have to be talking about your own self-righteousness, which you aren't supposed to approach Him with anyway, or be totally ignorant of the fact that you've been made righteous in your spirit with Christ's righteousness. Calling Jesus' righteousness—which you received at salvation—a filthy rag is an affront against God and His Word!

Isaiah 64:6 (filthy rags) was valid in the Old Testament because no one was born again; they didn't have new spirits. Regardless of how good they lived in their physical and soulish realms, they still sinned and came short of the glory of God. All of us have (Rom. 3:23). But now that you're born again, one-third of your being is completely righteous.

26

Unlike your spirit, your body and soul are in process. Until you're with Jesus in glory, they don't "arrive"—they just leave and head in that direction. Your physical, emotional, and mental realms will always need improvement, but your spirit is complete.

Since God is a Spirit, He looks at you Spirit to spirit (John 4:24). This is why you must worship Him in spirit and truth. You must come before Him in your spirit because it's the only part of you that's been created in righteousness and true holiness. God can only accept you based on who you are in your born-again spirit. That's why the new birth is so essential!

Anyone who hasn't received the Lord but tries to approach Him based on who they are in their actions and thoughts will always fall short of His glory (Rom. 3:23). Even if they've made significant personal improvements, God cannot lower Himself to their level. There's no way they can approach, communicate, or fellowship with God because of their unholy nature. Man's performance simply cannot accomplish what only the new birth can do—change his spiritual nature!

Fix Your Gaze

When you were born again, your old spirit died, was instantly removed, and replaced (Rom. 6). You became a brand-new creature with a recreated, elevated spirit. God literally sent forth the Spirit of His Son into your heart crying, "Abba, Father" (Gal. 4:6, Rom. 8:9). Your spirit and His Spirit intermarried, merged, and became one to create a totally new person. That's why God's mirror reflects you as righteous, holy, and pure. The makeup of your born-again spirit is identical to Jesus Himself!

Fix your gaze on God's mirror! Let your spirit's reflected image dominate your thoughts. As who you are in Christ grows stronger in your heart, carnal "reality" must give way to spiritual reality. That's when you'll experience life and peace!

Chapter 5

One With Jesus

As Jesus is, so are you—right now—in this world! **"Herein is our love made perfect, that we may have boldness in the day of judgment: <u>because as he is, so are we in this world</u>"** (1 John 4:17, emphasis mine). Notice how it's this world, not the next. The Word says now, presently, here on earth. It's not talking about heaven in the future! As Jesus is, so *are* you!

If you only look in your physical and soulish parts to see if you're like Jesus, you'll conclude, "The Bible is so hard to understand!" You see zits, baldness, wrinkles, bulges, and all kinds of other physical imperfections that you know Jesus doesn't have. In your emotional realm, there's depression, discouragement, anger, bitterness, and very little of God's kind of love. In light of these contrary facts, you could wonder, *How can I be as Jesus is?*

But now that you're beginning to grasp spirit, soul, and body, you know 1 John 4:17 must be speaking of your spirit. The born-again part of you is the only feasible explanation for "as Jesus is right now, so are you in this world!" It's not your body, nor your soul, but your spirit that's as Jesus is. What an awesome truth!

However, very few Christians truly believe this reality! Since their spirits can't be physically seen or emotionally felt, carnal facts consistently win over spiritual truth. Without looking at themselves in God's spiritual mirror, they just submit to what they see, taste, hear, smell, and feel. Most Christians remain carnally minded and experience its deadly effects instead of choosing to be spiritually minded and enjoying life and peace!

Hitting Pay Dirt

If you believed that you are, in your spirit, just as Jesus is right now in heaven—in all of His glory, power, and perfection—your life would be revolutionized! However, believing is just the first step. You must also learn how to release this reality from within. Just thinking this awesome thought once won't instantaneously change everything in your life. It's a process! As the seed of this truth becomes firmly rooted and established in your mind, a process of understanding, growing, and maturing begins in your soulish realm. Then, over time, you'll see radical changes manifest as you continue believing this truth and releasing God's corresponding power from within your born-again spirit.

What would you do if I told you there was a million dollars hidden in your front yard? It's buried (so you can't see or feel it), but it's there! Since nothing in the yard evidences this truth, all you'd have to go on is my word and your sense knowledge. Which would you believe?

If you trusted what you can see and feel more than my word, you'd miss out on the treasure. Why? You wouldn't pursue it! That money would stay buried, and you'd hardly ever think about it. Sure, someone might bring it up in conversation once in a while, but you wouldn't care. In fact, you could live in abject poverty just a few feet away from this abundant wealth hidden right there on your property. It could be that close, and you'd never benefit from it. Unless you believed my word, you'd do without the treasure!

However, if you trusted my word, you'd start digging! Although believing is an important step, it's just the first. You have to dig, find the money, and then bring it up out of the ground in order to benefit from it. If you had a steam shovel or a backhoe and could take bigger scoops, you'd be able to find the treasure quicker than someone with just a spoon. However, if both believed, both would eventually receive. You might get to it faster than the fellow with the spoon, but if he doesn't quit after going the first inch and getting a blister, he'll find the money too!

Even if all you've got is a spiritual spoon, you'll still hit pay dirt if you just keep digging. The more you know and understand God's Word, the quicker you'll start seeing spiritual riches manifest in your life. But before any of it works, you must acknowledge what's already there. In your spirit, as Jesus is, so are you in this world!

Embracing the Truth

You are one with Jesus Christ right now. **"But he that is joined unto the Lord is one spirit"** (1 Cor. 6:17). The Greek word translated "one" here means "a singular one to the exclusion of another." It's much deeper than mere similarity (i.e., being joined together as "one" in purpose); this speaks of complete union. If there are molecules and atoms in the spirit realm, then you are molecule-for-molecule and atom-for-atom identical to Jesus. As He is, so are you in this world. In your spirit, you are completely one with Him!

Many believers don't embrace these radical truths because they can't physically prove them. Trapped by natural perception, they're just too accustomed to being dominated by what they can see, taste, hear, smell, and feel to believe that they really do have this kind of spiritual unity with the Lord. Even though it's the truth of God's Word, they simply cannot bring themselves to perceive spiritual reality. It's just too contrary to their physical senses!

But you can believe and experience this truth! You can be transformed by renewing your mind to the point where you prove—manifest to your physical senses—the good, acceptable, and perfect will of God (Rom. 12:1-2). By embracing the Word, you'll be able to see the perfection that's in your spirit start flowing out through your soul and body. It'll not only impact you but also others whom God touches through you. Virtue will flow out of you and heal people just like it did with Jesus!

Since understanding these things, I've seen almost every kind of physical healing manifest (people raised from the dead, cancers healed, blind eyes and deaf ears opened, etc.). I've also seen emotional healing as people were set free from depression, discouragement, and the like. What I'm sharing with you works! It's not only changed my life but thousands of others I've ministered to as well!

I haven't tapped into all of it yet, but I've seen enough to testify! Like you, I'm still in the process of renewing my mind. But every believer has the potential of experiencing what I have and so much more! These truths will change you!

I Kept Digging

If you think what you can see, taste, hear, smell, and feel is all there is to reality, you won't be able to walk in all of God's will. You won't experience the power and ability of God within if you can't perceive things beyond your body and soul. If you think that God's power is with Him somewhere out there, eventually you'll become discouraged. It's not that you won't believe God has power, but you'll doubt you can ever attain it. You must believe you are one with Him in spirit and that it's your responsibility to release His power from within in order to see it manifest.

You can't doubt you'll get something that you know you've already got! It's just a matter of releasing what He's placed in you. If you really believe, you'll keep digging until you eventually hit pay dirt, and something begins to work!

I didn't understand how faith worked for many years, but just knowing it was there motivated me to keep digging. I began praying and believing for things when there was no natural evidence whatsoever that would lead me to think I could manifest such power. When I prayed for people to be healed, I didn't feel anything in my flesh—no tingle, no burning, nothing. I had no reason to believe God's power would manifest except that I'd been looking in my spiritual mirror and knew it was in me somewhere.

Not very many were healed at first because I didn't understand much. But since I laid my hands on so many different people, I started seeing some healed. Power would manifest that was beyond my natural ability. Encouraged, I kept digging. The deeper I dug, the more I'd find. The more I'd find, the quicker and easier it became to dig. I laid my spoon down in favor of a shovel. After awhile, I tossed the shovel aside and stepped up into a backhoe. Today, I'm still mining the riches God placed in my born-again spirit!

My attitude completely changed since discovering these truths. When problems came, I used to feel inadequate. I'd lament, "O God, I know You've got power, but I'm just a man. I don't have any power at my disposal." Then I realized I'm not just a man anymore. One-third of me is complete. One-third of me is identical to and one with Jesus. One-third of me is wall-to-wall Holy Ghost! Because of the confidence, security, and faith this has given me, I can confront and overcome problems now that I wasn't able to before. As you keep digging, these truths will do the same for you!

Chapter 6

Sealed!

No human being could have dreamt up the new birth and all of the realities that took place in our born-again spirits. It's just beyond our imagination that God would indwell us and that our spirits would be as He is in this world.

If you've received the revelation thus far, you can say, "I see it! I'm a brand-new person in my spirit. Old things passed away, and all things have become new. As Jesus is right now, so am I in this world. My spirit, the real me, was created in righteousness and true holiness."

Many people who have seen these truths, who rejoiced over them, and who were immediately impacted have since sinned or gotten busy and forgotten. Something happened and they find themselves back in some of the same negative situations they were in before being born again (i.e., defeat, discouragement, etc.). Due to their own apparent failure, they feel, *Maybe I was changed, but I've blown it...again.* Regarding everything we've discussed thus far about what happened at salvation, they argue, "That may have been so before, but I've blown it so much since then that it can't possibly be true of me now!"

I have good news—what God does in the spirit always remains constant and unchanging regardless of fluctuations in your performance!

Imprisoned

Inmates are descriptive of us all. Everyone has prisons—problems in their lives that keep them bound up. It's just that our problems aren't always quite as obvious as those of someone who's been placed behind bars.

In jail, many people realize that they've been ruining their own lives. No longer wanting the mess they have, they look around wondering, *How can I change? I need to get out of here!*

Then some minister comes across their paths preaching, **"Therefore if any man be in Christ, he is a new creature: old things are passed away; behold, all things are become new"** (2 Cor. 5:17). The thought that God loves them and wants to completely change their lives fits perfectly with what's going through most prisoners' minds. They desperately want to change, get out of there, and see their lives go in a different direction. So they pray and accept the Lord—not only for eternal benefit but for the purpose of immediate change as well.

A newly born-again prisoner will often become vulnerable to discouragement, doubt, and unbelief because they don't understand that the change took place in their spirit, and the rest of the Christian life is renewing their mind to believe and release what God has already put inside them. The next morning they wake up to find themselves in the same cell, facing the same trials and the same penalties. Looking only in the physical realm, it's easy for them to conclude, "It didn't work. The Word isn't true. God didn't change me because everything's still the same!"

This happens outside of jail too. Waking up the next morning, you find yourself still married to the same person, working the same job, facing the same sickness, and under the same mountain of debt. In fact, many times your problems intensify once you're born again. That's just the devil throwing everything he has at you because you're no longer on his side, and he wants to stop your witness. If you're not careful, you can become confused and think, *I'm not sure anything really happened!*

The change occurred in the spirit, not the physical realm. In fact, one-third of it is already complete! Your new man has been created in righteousness and true holiness (Eph. 4:24). You're not evolving into it because in your spirit, you already are.

Accepted

Jesus became sin so you could become righteous. **"For he hath made him to be sin for us, who knew no sin; that we might be made the righteousness of God in him"** (2 Cor. 5:21). Jesus became what you were so you could become what He is. He took your sin and gave you His righteousness!

Most of the church today acknowledges that Jesus paid the price for their sin but don't really believe they have become righteous. They think this takes place in the future when they arrive in heaven. Second Corinthians 5:21 refutes this misunderstanding by declaring He took (past tense) your sin *and* made (past tense) you righteous. If you believe the first half of this verse, then you ought to believe the second half too—you are righteous!

God doesn't look at you the way you look at yourself. He looks upon your spirit and sees that you are righteous. Most people

37

pray, "O God, I'm so sorry. I've failed You miserably again. How can You love me? Have mercy!" They don't recognize the truth that the performance of their bodies and souls, either good or bad, has absolutely no bearing on whether or not God accepts them. If you're born again, it doesn't matter if you've rebelled or just aren't everything you should be. God sees you as righteous and truly holy because He's looking at your spirit!

God is pleased with you! **"Having predestinated us unto the adoption of children by Jesus Christ to himself, according to the good pleasure of his will, To the praise of the glory of his grace, wherein he hath made us accepted in the beloved"** (Eph. 1:5-6). "Accepted" means more than just mere toleration. He's literally pleased with you! You might not be pleased with the shape your mind or body is in, but God sees you in the spirit. When you were born again, you became a brand-new creature, and He's pleased with His workmanship!

"Accepted" in Ephesians 1:6 is the same Greek word translated "highly favored" in Luke 1:28. **"And the angel [Gabriel] came in unto her [Mary], and said, Hail, thou that art highly favoured, the Lord is with thee: blessed art thou among women"** (brackets mine). These are the only two places in Scripture that this particular Greek word is found. Therefore, as the woman who bore Christ was accepted, so you are highly favored of the Lord!

Preserved & Protected

Once you believed, you were sealed with the Holy Spirit. **"In whom ye also trusted, after that ye heard the word of truth, the gospel of your salvation: in whom also after that ye believed, ye were sealed with that holy Spirit of promise"** (Eph. 1:13). Your born-again spirit was created in righteousness and true holiness (Eph. 4:24). As Jesus is, so became your spirit right here in this world (1 John 4:17). It became one with the Lord (1 Cor. 6:17). Then, all of this goodness was immediately sealed tight with the Holy Spirit.

When a woman cans food, she seals the jar with paraffin. This makes an airtight seal that preserves and protects the food within. Airborne impurities are prevented from getting inside and causing the food to rot and spoil. That's how this word "seal" is used in Ephesians 1:13!

When you were born again, your spirit was immediately encased—vacuum packed—by the Holy Spirit for the purpose of preservation. When you fail in any area of your life after being saved, the rottenness, uncleanness, and defilement that comes to your body and soul don't penetrate your spirit. This Holy Spirit seal keeps the good in and the bad out!

God doesn't look at sin the way people do. To Him, sin isn't only doing something wrong by violating a command, it's also not doing something right that you should have done. **"Therefore to him that knoweth to do good, and doeth it not, to him it is sin"** (James 4:17). Nobody loves their mate exactly like Christ loved the church. No one is as passionate about ministering to others as they should be. None of us meditates on the things of God as much as we could. Therefore, according to God's definition of sin, everyone constantly falls short!

If you don't understand that the Holy Spirit encased your born-again spirit, your conscience will eventually give you the impression that you've lost the righteousness and true holiness your spirit was created in. Your conscience, with its knowledge of right and wrong, constantly bears witness to your mind about your thoughts and actions. If you aren't careful, you'll allow the knowledge of your failures to affect you. You'll think, *Well, when I was born again, God gave me a brand-new start, but I've failed since then.* You may confess, try hard, and get back to where you feel like, *Now I'm back on track and everything's fine,* but it won't be long before your conscience shows you something else. If you go up and down like this day after day, year after year (which you do), after a while, you'll think, *What's the use?*

Born of God

However, the truth is that your spirit was sealed. Sin, and its effects, cannot enter into your spirit. When you sin, your spirit does not participate. It retains its original holiness and purity—and will for eternity! **"Whosoever is born of God doth not commit sin; for his seed remaineth in him: and he cannot sin, because he is born of God"** (1 John 3:9). This means you are as righteous and holy now, in your spirit, as you will ever be!

Many people struggle to understand 1 John 3:9 because its context clearly shows that Christians do sin: **"If we say that we have no sin, we deceive ourselves, and the truth is not in us"** (1 John 1:8). **"If we say that we have not sinned, we make him a liar, and his word is not in us"** (1 John 1:10). **"My little children, these things write I unto you, that ye sin not. And if any man sin, we have an advocate with the Father, Jesus Christ the righteous"** (1 John 2:1).

These are three instances from the same letter where the writer, the Apostle John, talks about sinning. The first two communicate, "If you say you haven't sinned, you're a liar." He adds, "I'm writing to you so that you will not (future tense) sin. But if you do sin, you have an advocate with the Father." Then, in 3:9 he declares, "If you're born of God, you cannot sin." That sounds very contradictory!

Both Scripture and experience reveal that Christians can sin. The context of 1 John shows that 3:9 isn't saying that it's impossible for a born-again believer to do something that's sin. Yet, it also clearly says that if you're born of God, you cannot sin. How can this be?

Big & Little Sins?

Some people take 1 John 3:9 to mean you can't "habitually" sin. Several Bible translations now even render it this way. People who think along this line preach: "If you were a drunk before you were saved, you might get drunk once or twice, but if you're truly saved, you won't habitually sin. Eventually, you'll see victory in that area, or you weren't truly born again."

In order to embrace this view, you have to categorize sin—which God doesn't. To Him, there are no "big" sins and "little" sins. By His definition, we all habitually sin. We all habitually fail to study God's Word as much as we should. We all habitually fail to love others the way we should. We all habitually fail to be as considerate as we should. We habitually get into self-centeredness, and God has to habitually deal with us about it.

Sometimes, we also pass over things that God calls sin. For instance, the Lord views gluttony the same as drunkenness, adultery, and murder (Deut. 21:20). Gluttony is a sin that can only happen habitually. You can't become overweight by eating just one large meal. Even if you gorged yourself, it would only make a pound or two of difference. In order to gain an extra fifty to a hundred pounds, you'd have to do it again and again and again. Being overweight is a habitual sin. This isn't to condemn anyone but to put things in perspective.

If you interpret 1 John 3:9 to mean that you cannot habitually sin if you're truly born of God, then nobody would qualify because we all habitually sin! The only way this can be preached is to say, "Well, you can't habitually do the 'big' sins, but the 'little' ones—yes, you can habitually sin." That's not what this verse is saying.

If you understand spirit, soul, and body, the interpretation of 1 John 3:9 is obvious. Your spirit is the only part of you that's been born of God. Your soul and body have been purchased, but not yet redeemed. Therefore, your spirit cannot sin even though your body and soul can. This means your performance doesn't affect the purity and holiness of your spirit!

This truth is pivotal to your relationship with God! If you tie His acceptance to your performance, you'll always come short. You might do better than certain other people, but your own conscience will condemn you. Eventually, it'll keep you from enjoying God's love and blessings because you know that you've tried and tried but still have faults after all these years. When you understand spirit, soul, and body, you know that it was your spirit that changed. Created in righteousness and true holiness, it's been sealed by the Holy Spirit so no sin can penetrate it. The righteousness you were born again with stays uncontaminated. Since God is a Spirit, He always deals with you Spirit to spirit. No matter how you're performing, you can always approach Him in your born-again spirit! That's awesome!

Chapter 7

Eternal Redemption

Hebrews 9 contrasts Old Testament Law with New Testament grace. What we've received through Jesus in the New Covenant is far superior to the Old. Old Testament sacrifices couldn't really set anyone free; they were put in place as an illustration and a reminder to the people until the real sacrifice came. Since they were symbolic and couldn't really purge from sin, Old Testament sacrifices had to be offered over and over and over again. But now that Jesus has given His life as *the* sacrifice for sin, it never again needs to be repeated. Through Christ, the perfect sacrifice for sin has been made once for all!

Your born-again spirit never needs to be re-cleansed, re-purged, or born again, again! **"But Christ being come an high priest of good things to come, by a greater and more perfect tabernacle, not made with hands, that is to say, not of this building; Neither by the blood of goats and calves, but by his own blood he entered in once into the holy place, having obtained eternal redemption for us"** (Heb. 9:11-12). Your salvation is eternal!

"For if the blood of bulls and of goats, and the ashes of an heifer sprinkling the unclean, sanctifieth to the purifying of the flesh: How much more shall the blood of Christ, who through the eternal Spirit offered himself without spot to God, purge your conscience from dead works to serve the living God? And for this cause he is the mediator of the new testament, that by means of death, for the redemption of the transgressions that were under the first testament, they which are called might receive the promise of eternal inheritance" (Heb. 9:13-15).

Jesus "entered in once into the holy place" and "obtained eternal redemption for us" (verse 12). Then, in verse 15, He provided an "eternal inheritance." Each of these statements emphasizes a one-time sacrifice that works once for all.

Once!

God really wants this point driven home to us! "For Christ is not entered into the holy places made with hands, which are the figures of the true; but into heaven itself, now to appear in the presence of God for us: Nor yet that he should offer himself often, as the high priest entereth into the holy place every year with blood of others; For then must he often have suffered since the foundation of the world: but now once in the end of the world hath he appeared to put away sin by the sacrifice of himself. And as it is appointed unto men once to die, but after this the judgment: so Christ was once offered to bear the sins of many; and unto them that look for him shall he appear the second time without sin unto salvation" (Heb. 9:24-28, emphasis mine). Old Testament sacrifices were offered constantly, but Jesus entered once into the holy place and made one sacrifice. Since we die just once, He suffered once, and that one sacrifice paid for sin forever!

Old Testament sacrifices could not do what the New Testament sacrifice of Jesus did. They were only temporary shadows of the real thing to come. **"For the law having a shadow of good things to come, and not the very image of the things, can never with those sacrifices which they offered year by year continually make the comers thereunto perfect. For then would they not have ceased to be offered? because that the worshippers once purged should have had no more conscience of sins"** (Heb. 10:1-2). If the Old Testament sacrifices really could have made the people perfect, they wouldn't have had to be offered over and over again. If they had worked, the worshipers—once purged—should have had no more conscience of sins!

New Testament believers need not be conscious of sin! The Old Testament sacrifices couldn't do it, but the New Testament sacrifice could and did. If you believe the truth of God's Word, you can literally reach a place where you are no longer sin-conscious. You would recognize that your spirit has been sanctified and perfected forever. God doesn't see you as a sinner; He sees your born-again spirit and is pleased. If you focus your thoughts on who you are in the spirit, you'll be conscious of righteousness!

This old phrase "I'm just a sinner, saved by grace" isn't true! If you're a sinner, then you need to be born again. If you were truly saved by grace, then you are no longer a sinner. Your spirit has been recreated in righteousness and true holiness and it cannot sin. Neither can it be penetrated by sin in your body or soul because of the Holy Spirit seal. Don't approach God confessing "I'm an old sinner." Draw near to Him boldly because you are now **"the righteousness of God in"** Christ (2 Cor. 5:21).

Approach God through Jesus and what He did in your born-again spirit, saying, "Father, thank You that through Christ I have boldness to enter right into Your very throne of grace because You have made me righteous!" If you honestly think, *O God, I'm so unrighteous!* then you either need to be born again, or you need to renew your mind and start believing the truth of God's Word. You've been made the righteousness of God in Christ Jesus!

Past, Present & Future

You've been forgiven of your sins—past, present, and future! That's what "eternal redemption" means. You might think, *God can't forgive me of a sin before I even commit it!* Well, you better pray that He can because Christ only died for your sins once. If Jesus can't forgive a sin before you commit it, then you can't be forgiven at all. Why? Jesus Christ hasn't died for sin in over 2,000 years!

Jesus paid for all sins—past, present, and future. Humans may not think this way, but God does. He's Eternal—time, distance, and space aren't problems for Him. Through His perfect sacrifice, God has already dealt with all sins!

When Jesus died, He put a will into effect. **"By the which will we are sanctified through the offering of the body of Jesus Christ once for all"** (Heb. 10:10). You were sanctified—separated, made holy—through the offering of Jesus Christ *once for all time*.

Generally speaking, Pentecostals were the ones who came up with this doctrine of backsliding, that every time you sin, you lose your salvation, and if you don't confess it before you die, you'll go to hell despite the fact that you've been born again for twenty or thirty years. They erroneously interpret this verse to mean "one sacrifice for all people."

However, the context proves that Hebrews 10:10 means one sacrifice made you holy for all time. Notice all the words referring to time in the next four verses. **"And every priest standeth**

daily ministering and offering <u>oftentimes</u> the same sacrifices, which can never take away sins: But this man [Jesus], after he had offered one sacrifice for sins <u>for</u> <u>ever</u>, sat down on the right hand of God; From <u>henceforth</u> expecting till his enemies be made his footstool. For by one offering he hath perfected <u>for</u> <u>ever</u> them that are sanctified" (Heb. 10:11-14, emphasis mine). Christ's one offering perfected and sanctified you forever!

In case you still aren't convinced, Hebrews 12:23 is another verse from the same context. **"To the general assembly and church of the firstborn, which are written in heaven, and to God the Judge of all, and to <u>the spirits of just men made perfect</u>"** (emphasis mine). How clear can it get? Your spirit has been perfected forever—all time. You don't lose your right standing with God if you sin. What a radical, wonderful truth for the church today!

David Saw It

Most Christians are taught that their performance affects their relationship with God. When you are born again, you're forgiven, cleansed, and you become a brand-new person. However, every time you sin, you lose that right standing with Him until you confess that particular sin and put it under the blood too. If you don't, God is displeased and cannot accept you. If you were to die before repenting and confessing all of those sins, you would go to hell. In a sense, they're saying you must be born again, again!

That's not what God's Word teaches! The Bible speaks of eternal redemption and eternal inheritance. You aren't sanctified and perfected only until you blow it—which is constantly. You're sanctified and perfected forever! People who believe they lose it all and have to start over again every time they sin will never really develop or see great growth in their spiritual lives. They're stuck in the flesh, focused on the performance of their bodies and their souls. God's Word reveals that your sins were forgiven—past, present, and future.

David saw by faith through the inspiration of the Holy Spirit just how great salvation would be. **"Even as David also describeth the blessedness of the man, unto whom God imputeth righteousness without works, Saying, Blessed are they whose iniquities are forgiven, and whose sins are covered** [past and present tense sins]. **Blessed is the man to whom the Lord will not** [future tense] **impute sin"** (Rom. 4:6-8, Paul quotes Ps. 32:1-2, brackets mine). Psalm 32:2 even adds, **"And in whose spirit there is no guile."** David (an Old Covenant patriarch) saw prophetically the blessedness of your New Covenant relationship with God. Because of your born-again spirit's righteous nature, the Lord no longer holds any sin against you.

Now that's good news!

Chapter 8

Standard Gospel Questions

Serious questions usually start coming right about now. "What are you saying? God will love me, and I won't lose my right standing with Him no matter what? Do you mean I can just go live in sin?" Paul dealt with this same thing! **"What shall we say then? Shall we continue in sin, that grace may abound?"** (Rom. 6:1). The answer, of course, is **"God forbid"** (Rom. 6:2).

Unless this question comes up, you aren't preaching the same Gospel as the Apostle Paul. He dealt with it four different times! "What am I saying? Do we continue in sin? God forbid!" Even though you have to explain what you mean, it should be a logical question.

Nobody interprets most churches today as saying "You can just go live in sin" because they're busy preaching so hard against it. This question never even comes up! Typical teaching today ties God's love and acceptance to your performance. Therefore, these messages given "in the name of the Lord" produce a works-righteousness (self-righteousness based on your actions) in most believers. The Bible doesn't teach that God accepts or rejects you because of your actions; it teaches that your actions can never be good enough!

God's Word says He accepts you based on whether your spirit is righteous or not. That spirit doesn't become righteous through your good actions and attitudes. Righteousness comes through confessing Jesus Christ as your Lord and Savior. As you are born again, God gives you this brand-new spirit. Righteousness is *NOT* based on your actions!

The next question people ask is, "Are you saying it doesn't matter how I live?" No, that's not what I'm saying. Paul continues in Romans 6 giving two reasons why a Christian should live holy: 1. Your new nature desires it, and 2. You don't want to give the devil access to your soul and body through sin. How you live doesn't affect your spirit's righteousness, but it greatly affects your life!

Sin's Strength

If you are truly born again, God has changed your nature. **"How shall we, that are dead to sin, live any longer therein? Know ye not, that so many of us as were baptized into Jesus Christ were baptized into his death?"** (Rom. 6:2-3). You are no longer a child of the devil who loves to sin. You do still sin, but it's not your nature anymore. Your spirit has been changed, and you no longer enjoy it. Every born-again believer has a built-in desire to live holy (1 John 3:3). You might not be fulfilling it, but it's there!

Preaching the Law—legalism and religious works—actually strengthens sin (1 Cor. 15:56). The Law makes you sin more by causing you to lust for the very thing that's forbidden. That's why God gave it! Mankind was being destroyed by sin, but we deceived ourselves into thinking, *I'm pretty good!* God answered, saying, "Oh, you think you're okay? Let Me show you what the real standard is." The Law made sin come alive so you'd recognize your need for a Savior (Rom. 7:9, Gal. 3:24).

Since I can't give a detailed explanation of this truth here, I'd like to recommend to you *The True Nature of God.* In that teaching, I expound much more on this particular point. You'll discover how God, who is the same yesterday, today, and forever (Heb. 13:8), can act so differently toward mankind from the Old Testament to the New. Without understanding how everything changed when Jesus Christ came, you'll think God is schizophrenic. I assure you, He's not!

The Lord's purpose in sending the Law was to make you bow your knee and confess, "God have mercy on me! I can't do it. I can't break this sin!" The Law wasn't given to help you overcome sin. It was to show you that sin had already overcome you! The Law actually strengthened sin and gave it so much power that it would effectively remove the deception that you could ever get rid of sin on your own. Religion, however, turns it around and says, "The Law was given to help you overcome sin." That's just not true.

If you're truly born again, you have a desire to live for God. **"And every man that hath this hope in him purifieth himself, even as he is pure"** (1 John 3:3). There will be varying degrees of this purity manifest in your actions and thoughts, but every born-again person seeks to purify themselves.

Sin gives Satan access to your body and soul. **"Know ye not, that to whom ye yield yourselves servants to obey, his servants ye are to whom ye obey; whether of sin unto death, or of obedience unto righteousness?"** (Rom. 6:16). Satan wants to bring death into your life any way he can—sickness, disease, poverty, shame, depression, discouragement, and all sorts of other nasty things. Why give your enemy an opportunity to come against you?

As a Christian, you don't have to live holy in order for God to accept and be pleased with you. However, your actions and attitudes do determine how you get along with other people. That's why it's still to your advantage to live a holy life!

Accidental Holiness

Knowing that I can relate to God based on the perfection, holiness, and righteousness in my spirit has set me free *from* sin—not *to* sin. In my flesh, I'll never be completely perfect until I receive my glorified body. Yet, in the meantime, I can go ahead and relate to God based on who I am in my spirit. This makes my relationship with Him stable and secure.

I've lived a holier life accidentally than most people have on purpose! Whenever these truths are taught, people criticize saying, "You're just preaching this so you can live in sin!" You can't accuse me of that because I've never spoken a word of profanity, drank liquor of any kind, smoked a cigarette, or even tasted coffee in all of my life! I'm not saying that coffee and booze are the same thing. There's scripture for drinking coffee. Mark 16:18 promises, **"If they drink any deadly thing, it shall not hurt them."** I'm just telling you that people can't look at me and say the reason I preach this is because it allows me to live in sin. No, I live a very holy life.

I don't live holy because I have to but because I want to. I don't do it in order to obtain God's blessing. I do it because He's revealed this truth to me and changed my heart. I desire to live holy because it's good for me. It helps me minister to others better, and it's happier to live holy than unholy!

God would still love me if I lived in sin (because my spirit is changed), but I wouldn't love me and other people wouldn't either. Sin offends God, but it also offends people. If you're truly born again, He'll deal with you as His child, based on your born-again spirit. But people won't love you if you steal from them. If they catch you, they'll throw you in jail where you'll suffer, be confined, and hurt. You won't have as nice of a life, but God will still love you. You'll still be righteous, but you'll also be stupid! (I'm not trying to be harsh, just blunt.)

Living holy doesn't make God love you more, but it does increase your love for Him. Likewise, a lack of holiness won't cause God to love you less, but it'll definitely decrease your love for Him. Although God's love for you doesn't change, your performance directly affects your love for Him. Can you see now God's purpose for holiness?

Come Boldly!

Sin is never a wise choice, but it's also never an issue between you and God. He dealt with your sin—past, present, and future—when you were born again. You can come boldly before the Lord at any time—even when you've fallen short, even when you're displeased with yourself, even when you've given Satan an inroad into your life. You can still come boldly into the very presence of God your Father and receive from Him because your spirit didn't lose any of its right standing with Him!

The Word encourages you to come before the Lord when you need mercy and help! **"Let us therefore come boldly unto the throne of grace, that we may obtain mercy, and find grace to help in time of need"** (Heb. 4:16). Don't just wait to come before Him until you've done everything "right." You can boldly approach the Lord and receive grace to help when you've totally messed things up. Your heavenly Father has invited you to draw near to His throne at any time by faith in His Son and who you are in Him. It's your birthright as a child of the King!

Chapter 9

Once Saved, Always Saved
or Born Again, Again?

When I first started understanding this revelation, I wondered, *God, is it like the Baptists say—once saved, always saved? Or is it like the Pentecostals teach—saved, lost, saved, lost, born again, again?* I struggled with these questions for a long time. Finally, the Lord spoke to me about it one day saying, "It's not A—once saved, always saved; or B—saved, lost, saved, lost, born again, again. It's C—none of the above!" He showed me that both positions have a partial truth, but the full truth is somewhere in between.

The "once saved, always saved" camp understands that your spirit is sanctified and perfected forever. Since you aren't saved by your own goodness, your lack of goodness can't un-save you. If you confess faith in the Lord Jesus Christ, you are born again. Since faith is the issue, sin doesn't cause you to lose your salvation.

Someone might say, "Now wait a minute! I believe if you sin, you lose your salvation. You can't tell me that a person who's committed some grievous sin can go to heaven!"

Even though I would be considered "holy" by most religious standards, I've fallen short in my actions. I haven't used profanity, drank liquor, smoked a cigarette, or committed adultery, but I've broken some of God's laws. I haven't loved people the way I should, neither have I always told the truth. I try to, but I remember being caught lying as a kid. I haven't committed what's considered "big" sins, but I've broken God's Law!

Plate Glass Window

"For whosoever shall keep the whole law, and yet offend in one point, he is guilty of all" (James 2:10). The Law is like a plate glass window. You could shoot a BB through it and make a little hole or throw a piano through it and make a huge one. Size makes no difference because the glass can't be patched. It's broken and must be replaced. If you violate one tiny command, you're guilty of breaking the whole thing!

You might not be transgressing all of God's commands, but you won't ever be able to do everything He's told you to do. Nobody always does all of the good they know to do (James 4:17). Therefore, everyone falls short.

Those who say "You have to be holy! You can't have sin in your life and still think you're saved" have to categorize it into "big" sin and "little" sin. They contend, "I'm talking about the big things. You can't tell me that a person who commits adultery and dies in a car accident on the way home with their sin not confessed would still be saved. Surely, they would go directly to hell. You can't tell me that an adulterer would go to heaven!" Forgive me for bursting your bubble, but that's religious tradition!

According to God's Word, there is no such thing as a "big" sin or a "little" sin (James 2:10). Speeding while driving is sin. Romans 13:1-7 instructs you to obey the laws of the land and to submit yourself to the governing authorities. Driving 56 in a 55 mph zone is breaking the command of God. If you break a little command, you are guilty of violating the entire thing.

The speeder is as guilty of sin as the adulterer. In man's eyes, there is a radical difference between going 1 mph over the speed limit and committing adultery. A speeder and an adulterer deserve different consequences in man's opinion, but in the eyes of God, sin is sin. Both come short of His standard of perfection. If you keep the whole Law and yet offend in one point, you become guilty of it all.

If the born-again believer who committed adultery and didn't confess it before dying goes straight to hell, then so does every believer who has ever sped. If that were true, then nobody would make it to heaven because we all come short and fail in many different ways!

Michael Jordan Vs. Couch Potato

If you've come short of the glory of God, you've missed it! Suppose you were in a room with a 20-foot ceiling, and God said you had to jump up and touch it in order to be saved. If you're Michael Jordan, you might be able to jump 15 feet high and get close. If you're a couch potato, you might only jump six inches and miss it by a bunch. Either way, the end result wouldn't be any different. If you can't touch the ceiling, you can't be saved. Both miss it!

That's the way it is with God's standard. He doesn't grade on a curve saying, "Do the best you can. As long as you're in the top 10%, I'll accept you, because you really tried." No, either you have to be perfect, or you need a Savior who is!

If you can sin your salvation away, then the only way to heaven is to die immediately after being born again. The loving thing to do with new converts would be to kill them. Then they wouldn't have a chance to sin and lose the salvation they just received. The evangelist who murdered them might go to hell, but the new believers wouldn't have time to void their ticket to heaven through sin. Sound ridiculous? It is!

Your spirit has been sealed, sanctified, and perfected forever. Its righteous state doesn't fluctuate with the holiness of your actions and attitudes. Since salvation depends solely upon putting your faith in Jesus and being born again, your sin doesn't affect your relationship with God. He fellowships with you based on your faith in Christ alone!

Renouncing & Rejecting

However, Scripture doesn't teach "once saved, always saved." Several places discuss the possibility of becoming reprobate and losing your salvation. The classic example is, **"For it is impossible for those who were once enlightened, and have tasted of the heavenly gift, and were made partakers of the Holy Ghost, And have tasted the good word of God, and the powers of the world to come, If they shall fall away, to renew them again unto repentance; seeing they crucify to themselves the Son of God afresh, and put him to an open shame"** (Heb. 6:4-6).

If a person falls away, there's no more sacrifice. Hebrews 6:4-6 is located in the same context, emphasizing how Jesus' one offering provided your eternal redemption. However, if that one sacrifice is voided, there isn't any other. It cannot be reapplied. You can't be born again, again. Jesus Christ is not going to suffer through that shame and humiliation to die a second time. His *one* sacrifice was it—forever!

You can make the sacrifice of Christ of no effect by turning to legalism and trusting in your own works for righteousness. **"O foolish Galatians, who hath bewitched you, that ye should not obey the truth, before whose eyes Jesus Christ hath been evidently set forth, crucified among you? This only would I learn of you, Received ye the Spirit by the works of the law, or by the hearing of faith? Are ye so foolish? having begun in the Spirit, are ye now made perfect by the flesh?"** (Gal. 3:1-3).

Salvation is both received and maintained by faith in Christ alone. **"Let us hold fast the profession of our faith without wavering"** (Heb. 10:23). You can't sin your salvation away, but you can renounce it. Rejecting your faith isn't easily done, but it is possible. Personally, I don't believe there are very many who do fall away.

Hardened

Before someone would ever renounce so great a salvation, they would have to become hardened toward God (Heb. 3:13-14). Although your spirit is unaffected by sin, your body and soul are. Sin dulls your perception, wisdom, and understanding of who you are in the spirit. If you persist in sin far and long enough, you can come to a place where Satan will try to make you renounce your faith in Christ. However, without being totally blinded to the truth, nobody in their right mind would ever reject the Lord!

If you renounce your faith and reject God, you can throw your salvation away. It's not something you just lose, like misplaced car keys. You must deliberately and openly reject it. That's something that takes place over a period of time.

You're saved by the grace of God, so sinful actions don't cause you to lose your salvation. However, sin can harden your heart until you eventually come to a place where *you* renounce your faith in the Lord (Heb. 6:4-6). If that happens, it's impossible to ever be renewed again to repentance!

This contradicts saved, lost, saved, lost; born again, again. Those who believe you lose your salvation every time you sin, also believe that all you've got to do is confess it and you're saved again. You just "pray through" and come back into right standing with God. Hebrews 6:4-6 says that can never happen! Either you didn't lose your salvation when you sinned, or if you did—you can never be saved again!

Do You Qualify?

The qualifications listed in Hebrews 6:4-6 are pretty stiff. You should look them over carefully before condemning yourself as reprobate. It's not talking about that time you were frustrated and said "I'm quitting! This doesn't work!" and then backslid into sin. No, it's much more involved than that.

In order to qualify, you have to (1) be enlightened, which means drawn by the Holy Ghost. John 6:44 declares, **"No man can come to me, except the Father which hath sent me draw him."** You couldn't have been coerced into making some statement, signing a church roll, or repeating a prayer. Then, after not experiencing a dramatic change, you became tired and renounced it saying, "I reject this. It's not real!" If this describes you, it wasn't a true conviction from the Holy Spirit. You were coerced, not drawn. You went to church because your parents made you, or you were dating someone who had you repeat a prayer. You don't qualify! Therefore, you aren't even held accountable for that so-called "rejection."

You also must have (2) tasted of the heavenly gift, which means you must be truly born again; (3) made a partaker of the Holy Ghost, which refers to being baptized in the Holy Spirit;

(4) have tasted the good Word of God, which means the Word has literally impacted you. You've done more than just put it in your mouth—you've swallowed it, digested it, and benefited from the nutrients and life in it; and (5) you've tasted the power of the world to come, which refers to a Spirit-filled person who has exercised the gifts of the Holy Spirit and is going on to maturity. In other words, you must be a mature Christian before you can actually renounce your salvation.

If a mature Christian rejects the Lord, they can never be brought back to a place of repentance. It's a one-time deal. They're held accountable, damned, and that's it!

Jesus proclaimed that blasphemy against the Holy Spirit was the one unpardonable sin (Matt. 12:31-32). Yet Paul said he obtained mercy because he **"did it ignorantly in unbelief"** (1 Tim. 1:13). This shows that even the unpardonable sin of blaspheming the Holy Spirit depends upon whether or not you did it knowingly.

You can't renounce your salvation ignorantly! That's what Hebrews 6:4-6 is saying. You have to be a mature Christian who was drawn by the Spirit, born again, baptized in the Holy Ghost, mature in the Word, and operating in the gifts of the Spirit before you can reject the Lord. Only then are you held accountable!

Too Young to Know Any Better

One time when I was a child, somewhere between five and eight, I became upset and ran away from home. I took off running but realized my mistake even before I lost sight of my house. *Where am I going? What will I eat? Where will I sleep? I love my parents!* I might have been angry, but I didn't want to run away. Being too proud to admit it, I got caught up in a barbed wire fence on purpose so my brother would catch me (he'd been running after me to bring me home).

Since I wasn't old enough, it wasn't held against me. Even though I was mad and had declared "I don't want to be a Wommack anymore!" before running away, it wasn't imputed unto me. If the police had been called, they would have been on my parents' side because I was so young. I didn't know what I was attempting, nor was I legally able to do it.

However, now I'm old enough to decide. As an adult, I could change my name and make a formal separation from my parents. If I renounced them, the government would back me up, and I could legally reject them.

It's the same thing with renouncing and rejecting salvation. God knows whether someone is mature or not. He alone knows their heart.

Beyond Hope

When someone rejects their salvation, they can never come back into relationship with God. **"And even as they did not like to retain God in their knowledge, God gave them over to a reprobate mind, to do those things which are not convenient...Who knowing the judgment of God, that they which commit such things are worthy of death, not only do the same, but have pleasure in them that do them"** (Rom. 1:28, 32). Giving them over to a reprobate mind, God takes away the conviction of the Holy Spirit.

"Reprobate" means "beyond hope." You aren't convicted of your need for relationship with the Lord unless the Holy Spirit is dealing with you (John 6:44). As long as He's dealing with you, you aren't reprobate. However, if someone fulfills the qualifications of Hebrews 6:4-6 and renounces their salvation, then God takes the Holy Spirit away and they become reprobate. Without conviction, they no longer know they're doing wrong. Not only do they like it, but they like all those who are in rebellion against God too. Reprobates display a total lack of desire and response toward the Lord.

Are you repenting and sorry for what you've done? Do you desire to be in relationship with the Lord? If so, you aren't reprobate. The Holy Spirit is still dealing with you. You weren't mature enough when you turned your back or fell away. Like Paul, you're forgiven because you were ignorant when you did those things. Praise God—He's your loving heavenly Father!

Chapter 10

Fullness Received

My spirit was created in righteousness and true holiness when I was born again (Eph. 4:24). Then, the Holy Spirit sealed this purity into my brand-new spirit (Eph. 1:13). Any sin I commit now in my physical actions cannot penetrate or contaminate my spirit because it's been sanctified and perfected forever (Heb. 10:10,14; 12:23). My born-again spirit cannot sin (1 John 3:9)!

I have received eternal redemption (Heb. 9:12). This doesn't encourage me to live in sin but instead gives me stability in my life and relationship with God. I live holy because I want to, and if I don't, I know I'll give Satan and other people an opportunity against me (Rom. 6:16). Living holy is definitely more beneficial than living in sin!

God is pleased with me because of who I am in the spirit (John 4:24). When I do fall short, sin doesn't have dominion over me the way it used to because I know now that God has already forgiven me completely—past, present, and future sins (Rom. 6:14). My spirit isn't stained in any way. Since God is a Spirit, I must fellowship with Him through who I am in the spirit.

My relationship with the Lord is constant. He's always loving me. He's always pleased with me—the real me, the born-again me, my spirit (Eph. 1:6). That's the part of me that God loves and that I've come to love. I'm not enamored with my carnal self and actions. I don't like some of what I see, do, and think, but I've come to realize there's a new me. In my spirit, I am thrilled with what Jesus has done, and I place my full confidence in that. Since I walk by the spirit, and not the flesh, I experience God's peace, joy, and life on a daily basis.

My life is stable. I don't feel like I lose everything every time I sin or fall short. I don't think that I need to be born again, again and start the whole growth process over. This concept of "one step forward and two steps back" is totally gone. When I do fail, I just turn from it. I repent and get back on track with what God's told me to do, knowing that I'm still who I am in Christ and infinitely more in my spirit than I've ever yet been able to appropriate and manifest. That's why I actively and aggressively continue renewing my mind to His Word.

Fruit Unto Holiness

"If we confess our sins, he is faithful and just to forgive us our sins, and to cleanse us from all unrighteousness" (1 John 1:9).

First John 1:9 has been traditionally taught that every time you sin, you have to confess your sins in order to receive forgiveness. If that's truly what it means, then this would put a tremendous burden upon you to deal with every sin. Religion categorizes sin, but God's Word is much more inclusive. Sin isn't only what you're doing wrong, it's also the right you failed to do. Some sins you realize, most others you don't. If you have to confess every sin before it's forgiven, nobody could retain their salvation. This just can't be what it means!

First John 1:9 refers to when you first come to the Lord. If forgiveness were dependent upon your confessing everything you've ever done wrong and failed to do right, salvation would be out of reach because you've forgotten too much. This verse instructs the unbeliever to be born again, not the believer to confess every sin all the time. It's how you first come to the Lord. You acknowledge your sin nature and separation from God in order to bow your knee and receive salvation. You confess that you're a sinner in need of forgiveness and are cleansed from all unrighteousness by receiving your brand-new, born-again spirit.

First John 1:9 can also mean cleansing the effects of sin from a believer's soul and body. Your spirit isn't affected by sin, but your soul and body are. Sin gives the devil a legal right to work his death into your life because you yielded yourself to him (Rom. 6:16). How do you repent of it and get him out? You say, "God, I was wrong and You were right. I sinned and gave Satan this opportunity. I repent!" By confessing, you take the salvation, the forgiveness, the holiness, and the righteousness that's already a reality in your spirit and never fluctuated when you failed, and draw it out into your body and soul. This literally drives the devil out and takes his place away. The enemy no longer has rights and privileges in your life once you repent and turn from what you've done!

If you understand your eternal redemption, you won't be emboldened to sin, but you'll be freed up to declare, "What a great God You are!" You'll want to spend even more time with Him. You'll desire to live holy so that nothing will ever dull you or keep you from perceiving these great truths and His love. Understanding your eternal redemption will cause you to live holy!

That's the way it should be! You shouldn't be trying to live holy out of fear of rejection and punishment; you ought to live holy as a result of your salvation. You should have **"fruit unto holiness"** (Rom. 6:22). Notice how it's a fruit, not a root, of salvation. "Holiness" doesn't produce God moving in your life, but your external actions of holiness are a result of understanding the righteous nature of your born-again spirit.

Never Separated From His Love!

This has changed my life! It's given me a deep abiding security in my relationship with God because I know He loves me! In fact, He loves me infinitely more than I've ever yet perceived. After the warm feelings of my miraculous encounter with God subsided, (because of my actions) I thought, *Well, He loved me at one time, but I'm not sure He still loves me now because I just don't feel worthy.* Then I came to realize that my born-again spirit is righteous and holy. I recognized that God looks at me Spirit to spirit, and He loves the born-again part of me!

I'm His workmanship, **"created in Christ Jesus unto good works"** (Eph. 2:10). In my spirit, I'm perfect and pure. God loves me and I'm never separated from His love. This sheds new light on, **"Who shall separate us from the love of Christ? shall tribulation, or distress, or persecution, or famine, or nakedness, or peril, or sword?...For I am persuaded, that neither death, nor life, nor angels, nor principalities, nor powers, nor things present, nor things to come, Nor height, nor depth, nor any other creature, shall be able to separate us from the love of God, which is in Christ Jesus our Lord"** (Rom. 8:35, 38-39). In my spirit, God has already given me His full measure of love. **"And of his fulness have all we received, and grace for grace"** (John 1:16). I'm full of God. One-third of me is wall-to-wall Holy Spirit! And if you're born again, all these things are true of you too!

This knowledge will impact your life and make you feel so pure. You'll be so appreciative of what God has done that you'll live holier in your actions accidentally than you've ever lived on purpose!

Chapter 11

God's Supernatural Faith

In your spirit, you have the complete measure of faith. You don't need more faith from God because you already have all you'll ever need. Your faith isn't small, immature, or in the process of growing; it's already as perfect and complete as the faith of Jesus. You just need to renew your mind and learn to release it!

When I first became serious about God, I started hungering to see in my life what I saw in the lives of Bible characters. When I read things in the Word, I knew they weren't just for the people back then. Even though I hadn't seen any of those things manifest prior to that time, I knew in my heart they were for me now too. Since faith is what releases the supernatural ability of God, I began a quest to start operating in His kind of faith.

Of course, I misunderstood a number of things at first. I thought faith was something to be obtained. I believed that I had to do things after being saved in order to make God give me more faith. Because of this, I felt my faith was inadequate every time I came up against a problem. I just embraced such recurring thoughts as, *Faith works, but I just don't have enough of it,* and, *What I've got is too puny!* That was my attitude. However, through this revelation of spirit, soul, and body, the Lord cleared up my misunderstandings about faith and revolutionized my life and ministry!

Faith Was A Gift Too!

Sometimes a passage of Scripture becomes so familiar that you can only see one application of it. Unless you allow the Holy Spirit to shine additional light on that part of His Word, you'll be stuck with only the understanding you already have. I'm not suggesting reading something into God's Word that isn't there, but I am recommending that you stay humble before your Teacher— the Holy Spirit—as we take a closer look at some very familiar scriptures (John 14:26).

The way you were born again is the way you receive everything in the Christian life—by grace through faith. **"For by grace are ye saved through faith; and that not of yourselves: it is the gift of God: Not of works, lest any man should boast"** (Eph. 2:8-9). Salvation is everything God provided through Christ's atonement; it's not just when you first walk through God's door by receiving forgiveness of sins and a brand-new spirit. Salvation is everything in His house as well—healing, deliverance, prosperity, joy, peace, love, anything you receive from Him. All these salvation benefits come the same way you were born again—by grace through faith!

Colossians 2:6 agrees, declaring, **"As ye have therefore received Christ Jesus the Lord, so walk ye in him."** How did you receive Christ? By grace through faith. How then do you walk in Him and enjoy all the benefits of His salvation package? By grace through faith!

Many people interpret Ephesians 2:8 too narrowly by limiting the word **"saved"** to mean only the initial born-again experience. However, the Greek word for salvation here is "sozo," which includes every aspect of salvation. Therefore, Ephesians 2:8 really says, **"For by grace are ye** *sozo—forgiven of sins, born again, made righteous, healed, delivered, prospered, etc.*— **through faith"** (emphasis mine).

Others miss the fact that it's not only salvation that is **"not of yourselves: it is the gift of God: Not of works, lest any man should boast"** (Eph. 2:8-9); it's also faith as well. God not only provides the salvation you need, but He also supplies the very faith you use to appropriate His grace! Both salvation and the faith to receive it are gifts from God!

God's Word Contains His Faith

You can't receive salvation without hearing the Word. **"So then faith cometh by hearing, and hearing by the word of God"** (Rom. 10:17). You might not hear it quoted chapter and verse, but the truths and concepts that are in God's Word must come across your path somehow. You need to know that Jesus died for your sins, and because of His love, He offers forgiveness independent of your actions. His only demand is that you believe.

Faith comes through hearing the Word. How? God's Word contains His faith. When you receive the Word into your heart, you're receiving God's supernatural faith. You must hear the Word because that's how you believe and receive.

God put His faith in His words. When those words are preached, they contain faith. If you will open up your heart, that faith will enter in and produce salvation (1 Pet. 1:23-25). The faith you use to receive salvation is not merely a human faith but God's own supernatural faith, which came to you through His Word.

It's important to know whether your faith is natural or supernatural. If you believe that your faith is just a human faith, the devil will be able to convince you that it's not very good. He'll tell you it's puny, weak, frail, and small in amount and strength. But when you understand that the faith you're using is God's supernatural faith, which was imparted to you through His Word, your level of confidence and expectation will rise. It's not only the faith you used to become born again, but it's the faith you use to appropriate everything in the Christian life!

Since God's faith is a supernatural faith, it produces supernatural results. It has the ability to do things that will take you beyond just the physical realm. If you believe you're using just a human faith for the Christian life, you'll only be able to receive natural results. However, when you realize that it's God's faith you're using, you'll start experiencing supernatural results!

Human Faith

Human faith is based upon natural knowledge. God created mankind as faith beings. Even before being born again and separate from the influence of God, there's still a natural kind of faith. In an attempt to explain faith, this was what my church taught me while I was growing up.

Taking a chair, they'd say, "How do you know if this chair will hold you up? It takes faith to sit in it." Then they'd add, "It's faith when you drive through a green light. You must believe that the other side has a red light. You don't know it because you can't see it, so you can't prove it. Even if the red is there, you still have to believe that the other cars will stop." And shifting to the skies, they'd say, "It's faith to ride in an airplane. You don't know how it works, and you aren't personally acquainted with the pilot. How can you be sure the mechanisms are correct and the pilot can work them?" They'd declare, "That's faith!"

It's a type of faith, but it's human faith. In other words, it's a faith based on sense knowledge—facts—things you can see, taste, hear, smell, and feel.

Whether you are conscious of it or not, the first thing you'd do before attempting to sit in the chair would be to glance over at it to see if it had all four legs. If it only had three legs and teetered like it was about to fall, you wouldn't sit in it. Whether you realize it or not, when you get ready to sit down in a chair, you inspect it. It might not be a perfect inspection, but you do gather some sense knowledge to base your action upon.

You've also been trained to know that when your side of the traffic light is green, the other side has red. You've got personal experience to base that upon because you've been on the other side waiting on the red many times before. However, for additional safety, you probably made sure nobody looked like they might speed through and run the light before you proceeded.

Human faith is limited to what it can see, taste, hear, smell, and feel. If you noticed that one of the wings was missing, you wouldn't fly on that airplane. If you saw a wreck at the intersection, you wouldn't just go right on through it, even if the light was green. If the chair looked like it would fall apart under your weight, you wouldn't try to sit on it. If the facts don't seem to support the action, you can't act contrary when you are using natural faith.

Your Faith Is Supernatural!

While human faith follows sense knowledge, supernatural faith precedes it. God demonstrated this kind of faith when He changed Abram's name to Abraham (father of many nations) before he even had a single child (Gen. 15:2-6, 17:4-6). **"(As it is written, I have made thee a father of many nations,) before**

him whom he believed, even God, who quickeneth the dead, and calleth those things which be not as though they were" (Rom. 4:17). This is how God's faith operates. He acknowledges those things which aren't yet manifest as if they already are. God calls those things as if they were, even before there is any physical proof of their existence. Natural faith can only acknowledge what it already sees, tastes, hears, smells, and feels. Supernatural faith literally brings things into manifestation from the spirit realm. Now that's a radical difference!

You used supernatural faith to become born again. It wasn't natural faith because you were believing for things that were beyond your sense knowledge. Unless you had a vision or heard an audible voice, neither of which is the norm, you couldn't perceive spiritual truth with your natural senses. You had to believe in things you couldn't see, like: heaven and hell, God and the devil, sin and forgiveness. All these were faith issues that could not be verified or proven by mere human faith. The Holy Spirit enlightened you from within as He spoke to your heart so you could take a step of faith that wasn't based on what you could see, taste, hear, smell, or feel. Through His Word, you were given God's supernatural faith when you were born again.

The same faith you used to become born again is now always present in your spirit. It doesn't evaporate, diminish, or get old and lose its power. That supernatural faith is exactly the same in your born-again spirit as it was the very moment you were saved. You may not be experiencing that faith and all of its benefits in your body and soul, but it's there in your spirit. If you've been born again, you already have the supernatural faith of God!

Faith is a fruit that stems from your spirit. **"But the fruit of the Spirit is love, joy, peace, longsuffering, gentleness, goodness, <u>faith</u>, Meekness, temperance: against such there is no law"** (Gal. 5:22-23, emphasis mine). Faith—belief—is a product from deep within the heart, not just the mind. **"For with the**

heart man believeth unto righteousness" (Rom. 10:10). For the born-again believer, faith has actually been put into your recreated spirit!

You don't need more faith—you just need to believe that you already have it. As Jesus is now, so are you in this world (1 John 4:17). Is Jesus in faith? Of course He is! He's operating in faith perfectly. Your born-again spirit has the faith of God in it perfectly, without lack or inadequacy. Acknowledge it! Go to God's Word and discover the laws that govern how faith works. Then, start cooperating and using them to your advantage. You'll find that the faith that's already inside you is more than sufficient for any problem you'll ever face!

Chapter 12

Like Precious Faith

You were justified by the faith of Christ. **"Knowing that a man is not justified by the works of the law, but by <u>the faith of Jesus Christ</u>, even we have believed in Jesus Christ, that we might be justified by <u>the faith of Christ</u>, and not by the works of the law: for by the works of the law shall no flesh be justified"** (Gal. 2:16, emphasis mine).

God not only provided salvation but also gave you the faith to receive it. You were so bound up in sin before being born again that you couldn't reach out in your own ability to receive the salvation God had already purchased for you. Your mind and heart were simply too corrupted to believe. This sin-caused blindness separated you from God. He pierced through your darkness by speaking His Word to you through someone. God's supernatural faith came with it. Then, when you embraced that Word in your heart, you used His faith to receive His gift of salvation.

Not only were you born again through that faith, but you're to live your entire Christian life by it! **"I am crucified with Christ: nevertheless I live; yet not I, but Christ liveth in me: and the life which I now live in the flesh I live by the faith of the Son of God, who loved me, and gave himself for me"** (Gal. 2:20, emphasis mine). It doesn't say *"I'm living by faith in the Son of God"* but rather *"I'm living by the faith of the Son of God."* (I am aware that several modern translations render it **"I live by faith in the Son of God,"** but that's not accurate according to the Greek.) Just a few verses earlier in 2:16, Paul stated twice that you are justified by the faith of Christ. It's very clear that it's not just a human faith that receives from God but His own supernatural faith.

Knowledge Problem

The first step is to believe you have this faith, but the goal is to release its benefits into your soul and body. Just like everything else in your spirit, your faith doesn't fluctuate because of your performance. You were born again, apart from your works, using the supernatural faith of God. Now, that faith is always there. Your faith begins to operate, work, become effective when you acknowledge the good things that are in you in Christ (Philem. 1:6). Acknowledge that God has already given you His supernatural faith!

You don't have a faith deficiency, you have a knowledge problem! You don't know what you've got. You haven't learned the laws that govern faith or how to cooperate with them. If you don't acknowledge this faith and learn how to use it, then you won't see it manifest. It won't be because you don't have it but because you're ignorant of how it works!

Every born-again believer has been given the measure of faith. **"For I say, through the grace given unto me, to every**

man that is among you, not to think of himself more highly than he ought to think; but to think soberly, according as God hath dealt to every man <u>the measure of faith</u>" (Rom. 12:3, emphasis mine). Some people teach and some Bible versions actually translate this incorrectly, saying <u>a</u> measure of faith. However, Galatians 2:16 & 20 both verify that this is truly <u>the</u> measure of faith.

You received the exact same quantity and quality of faith when you were born again as did every other Christian. However, in God's "soup line," most people think He dishes out faith using a wide variety of different measures. Someone's given a ladle full, another a teaspoon. To this one, a tablespoon, and to that one, barely a drop. Romans 12:3 soundly refutes this false perception. In reality, everyone's given the ladle full because it's <u>the</u> measure of faith!

Looking on externals, there's no doubt some people operate in more faith than others. You might think, *They've got more faith than I do!* No, they just have more of it out in the physical realm. In other words, they are using more of their measure of faith than you are. Let's say you and I were both given identical gift cards worth $1,000 each. I buy an $800 stereo system, and you purchase a $200 leather coat. Even though we were given the exact same measure initially, according to our use, we experience very different results!

Peter, Paul & You

Paul used the faith of Jesus. In Galatians 2:20, he basically stated, "I'm living by the same faith that Jesus used when He walked on this earth." Romans 12:3 reveals that there aren't varying measures or different amounts. So if Paul lived by the faith of the Son of God, then that means every other born-again believer like him also has the faith of the Son of God. What a radical truth!

When you were born again, you were given the faith of Jesus Christ. Even if you don't yet understand how to release it, just the knowledge that it's there and its potential would give you all the motivation you need to not quit until you see it manifest. If you could just grasp what I'm sharing, your expectation level would shoot through the roof!

Peter had this faith. **"Simon Peter, a servant and an apostle of Jesus Christ, to them that have obtained like precious faith with us through the righteousness of God and our Saviour Jesus Christ"** (2 Pet. 1:1). Peter wrote this letter to a group of believers who had already obtained this **"like precious faith."** It wasn't something they were searching for or seeking after; they already had it. Did they receive this faith by being holy and doing things? No, it came **"through the righteousness of God and our Saviour Jesus Christ."** When you were born again, you also received this **"like precious faith."**

Peter released his faith and manifested many awesome things! He walked on water in the midst of a raging storm (Matt. 14:29). He preached and saw three thousand people born again on the day of Pentecost (Acts 2:37-41). Peter healed the lame beggar at the temple gate (Acts 3:6-7). His shadow fell on people who were instantly made whole as he walked down the street (Acts 5:15-16). He also raised Dorcas from the dead (Acts 9:36-41). This is he who said you have like precious faith!

If you don't believe that you have this faith, then you might as well tear 2 Peter right out of your Bible because it doesn't apply to you! It's specifically written to believers with **"like precious faith"** (1:1). Peter wasn't operating in his own human faith. It wasn't because he was an apostle and had walked with Jesus that he was endued with such faith. Like Paul, Peter had been given the measure of faith upon being born again. He was living his life by the faith of the Son of God—and you can too!

Only Americans

You have the same faith as Jesus! You might not have all of it operating the way He did, but it's there. Your soul, like a filter, screens what flows out from your spirit into the physical realm. All of your thoughts and concepts that are contrary to the revelation of God's Word block the flow. The fact is, if your thoughts are really screwed up, very little of what's in your spirit will be able to pass through your soul and manifest. That's why you may not be seeing much happen as far as actions and results. However, as you continue renewing your mind, more of God's supernatural faith that's in you will be free to manifest!

I've experienced a tremendous increase of God's faith manifest in my life. Although I'm not a perfect example, I've seen people rise from the dead. Blind eyes and deaf ears have literally opened right before my eyes. The gifts of the Holy Spirit have been able to flow through me far beyond anything I could have ever perceived in the natural realm. Through a word of knowledge, I've actually told individuals their names before! I've also accurately perceived in my spirit different people's sicknesses and diseases, what's going on in their marriages, etc. It takes faith to do such things! I don't manifest it perfectly, but I've seen such an increase that I can tell you about the positive results I've experienced, all because I've believed that I already have God's supernatural faith. I'm not trying to get more faith—I'm just learning to release what I already have!

When asked on television "Why do you see so many more healings in Third-World countries than here in the United States? Is it because they have more faith?" Reinhard Bonnke, renowned German world healing evangelist with a special passion for Africa, answered, "That's an invalid question!" He clarified his assertion by adding, "Americans are the only people on the face of the earth that I have encountered who have this concept of 'more faith' and 'little faith.' In other countries, either you believe or you don't! Only Americans believe in varying degrees and having to hit level 10, 20, or whatever before their faith starts to work. Really, this idea violates what Jesus taught in Matthew 17:20. He said that if your faith was like a grain of mustard seed, you could tell a mountain to move, and it would obey you. You could just speak to it, and your faith would work!"

What a difference this revelation will make in your life! You can now honestly and boldly declare, "I was given **the** measure of faith from Jesus at salvation. The faith of Christ is in me—no more and no less than any other born-again believer. The same faith Jesus used to raise Lazarus from the dead is available to me right now. It's just a matter of renewing my mind because in my spirit, I've got the same power, anointing, and potential. From this day forward, I expect to see an increase of manifestation in my life to the glory to God! Amen!"

Chapter 13

Your Spirit Knows All Things

Your born-again spirit came with the mind of Christ. **"For who hath known the mind of the Lord, that he may instruct him? But we have the mind of Christ"** (1 Cor. 2:16). In your spirit, there's a mind that already knows all things. The rest of the Christian life is learning how to draw it out into the physical realm. When that happens, you experience what's called "revelation knowledge."

You were born with a natural mind. It operates both in the soulish realm and in the physical realm as your brain. When you came into this world, you didn't know anything. Your brain had some automatic functions that kicked in, like breathing, pumping blood, etc., but your mind had to be educated. You didn't come out of the womb walking and talking. You had to train yourself to coordinate your muscles. This required lots of input!

When you were born again, you received the mind of Christ in your spirit. However, your spirit mind doesn't have to be developed, trained, or taught because it was born again in perfect knowledge.

You might be wondering, *What about 1 Corinthians 13:9-10, which talks about only knowing in part until that which is perfect is come?* That's referring to your natural mind in your soulish realm. Right now, you don't understand everything with your physical mind. You are in the process of renewing it, which won't be complete until you receive that which is perfect—your glorified body. But in your spirit, you have the mind of Christ, which is already complete. It's just not manifest in your limited little brain inside your skull!

Nobody can defend the erroneous position that 1 Corinthians 2:16 means you have the mind of Christ right now in your physical mind. There are things the Lord Jesus knows that you simply aren't aware of in your natural mind. The Lord knew what He was saying in the Word, but you and I are still discovering the fullness of His meaning—even in just the Gospels alone! Nobody can claim total understanding and complete revelation because your actions and attitudes don't back it up.

Are You Double-minded?

Your spirit mind and physical mind are two separate entities within you. When they don't agree, double-mindedness occurs. **"Purify your hearts, ye double minded"** (James 4:8). The key to the Christian life is training your physical mind to agree with your spirit mind, which is the mind of Christ.

You are spirit, soul, and body. Your born-again spirit always agrees with God. Your body is under the influence of what it can see, taste, hear, smell, and feel. When your natural mind thinks the same way as your spirit mind, you're single-minded. That's when you are believing with all your heart and see God's power manifest. However, if your physical brain thinks contrary to your spirit mind, your experience will be different than the way your spirit thinks. Your soul—specifically your natural mind and the way you think—is the determining factor.

Your spirit mind always thinks the way God thinks. The Word perfectly represents what you think in your spirit. It's saying, **"I can do all things through Christ which strengtheneth me"** (Phil. 4:13). If your physical mind agrees, then you'll see supernatural power and ability flow through your soul into your body, which produces results in the physical realm. But if your mind is contrary, thinking *I can't beat this sickness. I've known five people who've died of this same thing, and my doctor told me it's hopeless!* then you're double-minded. A double-minded person receives nothing from the Lord!

Single-mindedness brings stability, but double-mindedness causes instability. **"If any of you lack wisdom, let him ask of God, that giveth to all men liberally, and upbraideth not; and it shall be given him. But let him ask in faith, nothing wavering. For he that wavereth is like a wave of the sea driven with the wind and tossed. For let not that man think that he shall receive any thing of the Lord. A double minded man is unstable in all his ways"** (James 1:5-8). The mind of Christ is in your spirit, but your soul doesn't automatically think that way. It takes effort to renew your physical mind to agree with your spirit mind. Basically, this is where the conflict in the Christian life is—in the mind.

You Know All Things

Most Christians believe that the only thing that changed when they became born again is their future—heaven instead of hell. After accepting Christ, they didn't see any change in their physical bodies, and they didn't automatically perceive it in their souls either, so they conclude that the real change must just be on paper. Nothing really changes until heaven, when everything will be awesome.

Yes, the change will be completed in heaven, but right now one-third of you is already complete. Your spirit has the mind of Christ and knows all things! If you really believed this, you wouldn't be so easily pushed into defeat, whining, "I know God can do it, but I just don't understand the things of God!" Embracing your ignorance, you sing songs about someday it'll be better, but now "I'm just a poor wayfaring pilgrim." Wailing and travailing, you glorify your infirmities, taking solace in the fact that "I'm just so inadequate. I can't experience victory until I go to be with the Lord." That's not true! You just don't realize that in your spirit, you're already a brand-new person!

In your spirit, you know all things! **"But ye have an unction from the Holy One, and ye know all things"** (1 John 2:20). "Unction" simply means "an anointing, a special enduement with power, or an ability." The Holy One is Jesus.

People who don't understand spirit, soul, and body read a verse like this and throw up their hands saying, "The Bible is so hard to understand! I can prove by my last test score that I don't know all things. I even forgot where I put my keys this morning. After walking into the room, I couldn't remember why I was there. That proves I don't know all things!" Those who only acknowledge their physical brain and soulish realm will never be able to embrace this truth from God's Word.

However, 1 John 2:20 plainly reveals that you know all things. How can this be? In your spirit, you have the mind of Christ. The Greek word for "all" means "to the exclusion of nothing." This means you not only know some things or many things but <u>all</u> things. In your spiritual mind, you know everything Jesus knows!

The Road to Manifestation

You're probably asking, "That's great, but what good does it do me? How do I get it out into the physical realm where I need it?"

First and foremost, you must believe you've already got it. You can't release something you don't really believe you have. If you waver regarding the truth that your born-again spirit has the mind of Christ and knows all things, then as you put forth effort in the process of releasing this, the devil will tempt you to think, *What that guy said isn't true. The Word doesn't mean that. This just doesn't work!* Unless you're absolutely convinced, you'll get frustrated and quit before you see the manifestation. You must believe you have the mind of Christ in your born-again spirit, even if you mess up. That's the first step.

Once you truly believe, you're on the road to manifestation!

Chapter 14

Releasing the Mind of Christ

Studying God's Word will draw out the wisdom that's in your spirit. When you're reading the Bible, you are receiving words with your physical eyes that are spirit and life. As you take this knowledge into your soul, new thoughts and ideas come to your physical mind. When this happens, your spirit—which already has the truth and mind of Christ—will bear witness with it.

Surely you've read a scripture and felt like all of a sudden you "saw" it. You may have read it a dozen, even a hundred times, before, but all at once, everything within you shouts, "Yes!" That's your spirit and your soul becoming of one mind. When your soulish realm gains a truth and begins to embrace it, your spirit connects and agrees. Once the connection is made, that truth just goes off inside of you. It's now revelation and reality to you. Because of your inner witness, you don't necessarily need anyone else to prove it; you just know!

Several scriptures reveal this inner witness. **"The Spirit itself beareth witness with our spirit, that we are the children**

of God" (Rom. 8:16). First John 5:6-10 also describes this, specifically verse 10, which says, **"He that believeth on the Son of God hath the witness in himself."**

Studying God's Word is vital for achieving single-mindedness and releasing God's power! Your spirit mind, the mind of Christ, agrees completely with the Word. When a truth from God's Word takes root in your soulish realm, that same knowledge, which has already existed in your spirit mind, rises up and meshes with it. This draws God's power resident within you out into the physical realm. That's when you see manifestation!

Your Spirit Prays!

Praying in tongues is another powerful way to release the mind of Christ. **"Follow after charity, and desire spiritual gifts, but rather that ye may prophesy. For he that speaketh in an unknown tongue speaketh not unto men, but unto God: for no man understandeth him; howbeit in the spirit he speaketh mysteries"** (1 Cor. 14:1-2). When you pray in the Spirit, you are speaking mysteries.

Your spirit prays! **"For if I pray in an unknown tongue, my spirit prayeth, but my understanding is unfruitful"** (1 Cor. 14:14). This scripture shows both minds in operation. When you pray in tongues, your spirit prays, but your understanding—your soulish, physical, natural mind—is unfruitful.

You build yourself up by praying in tongues. **"He that speaketh in an unknown tongue edifieth himself"** (1 Cor. 14:4). "Edify" means "to build up" or "to promote spiritual growth." It's your soul that's actually growing and being built up because your spirit is already perfect and complete. The mind of Christ in your spirit prays when you pray in tongues.

Your goal is to facilitate single-mindedness. You aren't trying to get the Word of God into your spirit because the mind of Christ already knows all things. You are trying to get God's Word into your soul so that your spirit can bear witness with it. As your soulish realm embraces a truth and agrees "Yes God, this is what I believe. I'm throwing out all other contrary thoughts and belief systems. This truth will now rule my life," you become of one mind. Your soul unites to your spirit's way of thinking, and you're built up by drawing your spirit's wisdom and knowledge out into the physical realm. That's when you'll see God's power manifest!

Hidden Wisdom

When you pray in tongues, your spirit prays the hidden wisdom of God. **"Howbeit in the spirit he speaketh mysteries"** (1 Cor. 14:2). What are those mysteries? **"The wisdom of God in a mystery, even the hidden wisdom, which God ordained before the world unto our glory"** (1 Cor. 2:7). That's what the Apostle Paul preached!

In 1 Corinthians 2, Paul describes his preaching and wisdom. He didn't just use his human intellect but ministered God's Word **"in demonstration of the Spirit and of power"** (1 Cor. 2:4). In the process of explaining this, Paul actually put down carnal knowledge—learned physical knowledge, the kind you receive from school—in favor of God's wisdom. In other words, there's a wisdom that proceeds from your born-again spirit (mind of Christ, 1 Cor. 2:16), and there's a wisdom that comes from your physical brain (what somebody taught you). Since you cannot really understand the things of God with just your natural mind, you must understand them through your spirit man. It's this wisdom that comes from your spirit that enables you to relate to God. Paul preached this wisdom as he invited unbelievers to believe and as he encouraged them to mature.

"But God Hath Revealed..."

Before moving on, I'd like to clear up a misuse of 1 Corinthians 2:9, which says, **"But as it is written, Eye hath not seen, nor ear heard, neither have entered into the heart of man, the things which God hath prepared for them that love him."** Some people read that and say, "This contradicts what you're teaching. It shows that you can't really know the things of God. This verse proves that He's mysterious and you can't really know!"

Don't stop there! Keep reading the next few verses: **"<u>But God hath revealed them unto us by his Spirit</u>: for the Spirit searcheth all things, yea, the deep things of God. For what man knoweth the things of a man, save the spirit of man which is in him? even so the things of God knoweth no man, but the Spirit of God. <u>Now we have received</u>, not the spirit of the world, but <u>the spirit which is of God; that we might know the things that are freely given to us of God...we have the mind of Christ</u>"** (1 Cor. 2:10-12, 16; emphasis mine).

First Corinthians 2:9 contrasts Old Testament saints, who couldn't understand, with New Covenant believers, who know all things in their spirits! In this verse, Paul quoted an Old Testament scripture (Is. 64:4). Old Covenant people weren't born again, so they didn't have born-again spirits. Because of this, it's totally accurate to say that they couldn't understand the things of God. To them, it's foolishness because they have to be spiritually discerned (1 Cor. 2:14). However, it's inaccurate to say the same thing about a New Testament believer who has the mind of Christ in their born-again spirit. You can understand the things of God!

Paul preached the hidden wisdom of God that he received by revelation. He declared, **"I speak with tongues more than ye all"** (1 Cor. 14:18). As Paul prayed in the spirit, he spoke forth God's mysteries and received revelation knowledge concerning them (1 Cor. 14:2). However, he did not preach or teach in tongues (1 Cor. 14:19). Paul ministered in his native language the wisdom he received through praying in tongues.

Inside Out

Pray in tongues when you study God's Word. As you do, you'll release the mind of Christ into your soulish realm through revelation knowledge. I'm not advocating speaking in tongues and then just accepting whatever comes to mind as being from God. No, it should line up with the Word. God will supernaturally reveal things to you through His Word as a result of praying in tongues.

Revelation knowledge comes by the Holy Spirit inside your born-again spirit bearing witness in your soul with a truth from God's Word. You might be reading or listening to Scripture when suddenly, it comes alive inside. That's revelation!

Simeon recognized the Christ Child by revelation knowledge. **"And it was revealed unto him by the Holy Ghost, that he should not see death, before he had seen the Lord's Christ. And he came by the Spirit into the temple: and when the parents brought in the child Jesus...Then took he him up in his arms, and blessed God"** (Luke 2:26-28). No human could have told him these things. God revealed it to Simeon through his spirit.

Revelation knowledge comes from the inside out, not the outside in. You may be reading the Word, studying it, looking things up in the Greek, checking cross-references, and reading or listening to someone else's opinion of what the Word says. But then, all of a sudden, the mind of Christ in your born-again spirit just reaches up from inside and grabs that truth shouting, "Yes! This one's true. This one is for you!" That's revelation knowledge.

Believe to Interpret

When you pray in tongues, you can believe God for interpretation. **"Wherefore let him that speaketh in an unknown tongue pray that he may interpret"** (1 Cor. 14:13). I admit that the context of this verse primarily addresses the need for interpretation of a publicly given tongue in a church service, but you can believe God for interpretation when you're praying in the spirit privately as well.

Praying in tongues benefits you whether you believe for interpretation or not. It relieves stress and releases the peace of God into your soul and body. **"For with stammering lips and another tongue will he speak to this people…This is the rest wherewith ye may cause the weary to rest; and this is the refreshing"** (Is. 28:11-12). It builds you up and promotes spiritual growth (1 Cor. 14:4). Since you are praying from the mind of Christ, why wouldn't you want to interpret?

I started interpreting my speaking in tongues a long time ago. When I first fell in love with the Lord, I went through an intense time of excitement, anointing, and stirring within, but my mind couldn't comprehend it. Then in Vietnam, I began seeing little glimmers of truth while studying the Bible. After returning home and marrying Jamie in October 1972, I really started poring over the Word. Scriptures began coming alive to me, and my spirit would rejoice. I'd read certain passages, and the spirit inside me just wanted to stand up and shout! However, since this was contrary to the religious way I'd been taught, I really struggled with it.

In my heart, I determined to break through. For an extended season of time, I spent six to ten hours a day writing scriptures out longhand on my legal pad. Along the way, I stopped and meditated on each individual word. Then I locked myself in the closet of our little apartment in Garland, Texas (a suburb of Dal-

96

las), to pray in tongues over these scriptures for an hour or two. My spirit already knew these truths, but as I prayed in tongues and asked God to interpret them to my mind so I could understand them, revelation came.

Understanding came as I wrote these scriptures out, meditated, prayed in tongues over them, and received interpretation. In fact, this revelation of spirit, soul, and body was one of the first things He showed me. Since my thinking had been so screwed up from religion and wrong teaching, it actually took a couple of months before I started making the connections. Then all of a sudden, in what seemed like one week's time, God started putting some of this together for me. I understood about eternal redemption and how God could love me. These truths exploded within and became reality to me. After about a week of this, the revelation was coming so fast and furious that I literally had to ask God to slow it down. I wanted to comprehend and retain it all without missing a single thing. One of the ways this happened was I prayed for interpretation!

Disaster or Safety?

Now, just because you pray in tongues and ask God for interpretation doesn't mean you should accept any and every thought that comes to your mind as being from God. That's a recipe for disaster! You must judge every thought by the Word of God. The Spirit and the Word always agree (1 John 5:7). They never disagree because God's Word never contradicts spiritual truth. Whether you are praying in tongues and believing for interpretation or not, whenever thoughts that are contrary to the Word flash across your mind, you should immediately conclude "That's not God!"

Paul rebuked the Corinthians for using the gifts of the Holy Spirit carnally. His comments in 1 Corinthians 12, 13, and 14 were corrections regarding the proper use of the gifts, especially speaking in tongues. Therefore, just because you are praying in tongues, it doesn't guarantee that they are completely pure and fully inspired by the Holy Spirit. Your flesh could be a factor.

However, if you stay within these biblical boundaries, you'll be able to safely receive much revelation from the Lord. As you pray in tongues and ask for interpretation, thoughts will come, and all of a sudden you'll say, "I've never seen that before!" Then, as you verify it in more than just one obscure place in the Bible, it'll become an obvious truth to you.

Basically, you need to know God's Word to be able to do this. This may not be the way an immature Christian should operate. I was spending six to ten hours a day studying the Scriptures and then one or two hours praying in tongues for revelation. I don't think you ought to spend one hour studying the Word and then many hours praying in tongues. It ought to be the opposite—many hours in the Word. Through this, God has revealed many things to me!

These truths on spirit, soul, and body came through God's Word. Everything I share, I share from Scripture. But the reason these verses and passages have come alive and impacted my life in ways they might not have for you is because I mixed my Scripture meditation with praying in tongues.

For additional information, my teaching entitled "Revelation Knowledge" goes much further in depth on this topic. I elaborate on many things that I've only been able to touch on here, including how to interpret, checks and balances, etc. I encourage you to get a copy!

Meditating God's Word, speaking in tongues, and receiving interpretation is the fast track to single-mindedness and manifestation!

Chapter 15

Empowerment Required

God has imparted perfect wisdom and complete revelation into your born-again spirit. **"Wisdom is the principal thing; therefore get wisdom: and with all thy getting get understanding"** (Prov. 4:7). Wisdom and understanding are keys that will unlock anything else in life you need. Therefore, draw on that wisdom and receive understanding so the floodgates of your soul will open up to allow God's truths already in your spirit to manifest in the physical realm. Yes, you can live a fruitful and fulfilled Christian life!

Without the empowerment of the Holy Spirit, you won't be able to fully release all of these wonderful realities already present in your born-again spirit. That's why the baptism in the Holy Spirit is so important!

Jesus needed the baptism in the Holy Spirit! He was born as God in His spirit and as man in His soul and body. He was complete in His spirit while on the earth in His physical body. However, Jesus didn't do any miracles until He received the baptism in the Holy Spirit (Luke 3:21-22, 4:1,14 & thereafter).

Since the Father, Son, and Holy Spirit are One, they don't operate independent of each other. The Holy Spirit is the One who releases the wisdom and revelation of God. He comforts, teaches, and reminds. **"But the Comforter, which is the Holy Ghost, whom the Father will send in my name, he shall teach you all things, and bring all things to your remembrance, whatsoever I have said unto you"** (John 14:26). He guides into all truth, listens, speaks, shows things to come, glorifies Jesus, receives of Him, and shows it by revelation to you! **"I have yet many things to say unto you, but ye cannot bear them now. Howbeit when he, the Spirit of truth, is come, he will guide you into all truth: for he shall not speak of himself; but whatsoever he shall hear, that shall he speak: and he will shew you things to come. He shall glorify me: for he shall receive of mine, and shall shew it unto you"** (John 16:12-14). Apart from the Holy Spirit, you won't have access to all that God has placed within you!

Receive His Spirit & Pray In Tongues!

When you receive the baptism in the Holy Spirit, the ability to pray in tongues comes with it. As you pray in the Spirit, you draw on and release the wisdom that's in the born-again part of you. It's not the only way, but it's certainly one of the primary ways. Therefore, it's essential that you receive the baptism in the Holy Spirit!

The baptism in the Holy Spirit is a second, separate experience from salvation. You receive an enduement of power by the Holy Ghost and the gift of speaking in tongues, which will help you operate this power. When you pray in tongues, you build yourself up, but it's much more than just an emotional lift. It helps you release the wisdom of God within you. Even if there were no other results (which there are), that would certainly be enough! Speaking in tongues produces tremendous spiritual benefits!

Some groups overemphasize speaking in tongues when you first receive the baptism in the Holy Spirit and underemphasize the benefits to your Christian life thereafter. Due to this, many who have received the baptism in the Holy Spirit only spoke in tongues once or twice to prove they had it. However, they didn't know there were other benefits, so they haven't really used the gift since. They also have been missing out on the tremendous benefits speaking in tongues brings to their daily lives.

I expound much more from God's Word on these topics in my messages entitled "What Is the Baptism of the Holy Spirit" and "Speaking in Tongues" (collectively known as *The Holy Spirit* teaching). If you aren't baptized in the Holy Spirit and speaking in tongues, I encourage you to get this teaching because you're really missing out. In fact, you're probably frustrated and powerless in your Christian life. Receiving the Holy Spirit will help you experience His love more than ever before and make His power available to you. Besides, the Lord Jesus Himself commanded, **"Receive ye the Holy Ghost"** (John 20:22). Will you obey?

If you are reading this book and haven't yet received the baptism in the Holy Spirit, you need to! Either go to someone who already has, or directly seek the Lord in prayer about it. I encourage you to call our Helpline because someone will be happy to explain and pray with you to receive. We see many, many people baptized in the Holy Spirit and speaking in tongues over the phone!

As you speak in tongues, your spirit prays, and the perfect mind of Christ releases the hidden wisdom of God. Then, ask and believe for interpretation (1 Cor. 14:13). Let God give you understanding so that revelation knowledge of the mysteries you are speaking in the spirit can come out into your physical mind. That's when you'll see His power manifest!

Chapter 16

Spirit vs. Flesh

Once you're born again, the rest of the Christian life is learning to walk in the spirit. It's letting what God has done through the new birth dominate you more than your physical, emotional realm. That's really how simple the Christian life is!

It may be simple, but it's not easy! One of the hardest things you'll ever do is learn how to turn from your natural self-rule and let who you are in Christ dominate instead. Why is it so difficult? You must perceive your spirit by faith in God's Word because you can't see or feel it. Jesus' words are spirit and life (John 6:63). When you look into God's Word, you're looking into a spiritual mirror (James 1:23-25). The only way to really know what is true about who you are in the spirit is by believing God's Word. You must shift from walking by sight (sense knowledge) to walking by faith (revelation knowledge) (2 Cor. 5:7). All you have to do is start basing your thoughts, actions, and identity on who you are in Christ.

As long as your flesh is contrary to your spirit, you'll have conflict. **"This I say then, Walk in the Spirit, and ye shall not fulfil the lust of the flesh. For the flesh lusteth against the Spirit, and the Spirit against the flesh: and these are contrary the one to the other: so that ye cannot do the things that ye would. But if ye be led of the Spirit, ye are not under the law"** (Gal. 5:16-18). "Contrary" means they're "opposed, enemies, adversaries." This conflict between spirit and flesh is your true spiritual warfare!

Each and every day of your life, the battle lies in whether you'll be dominated by your flesh or your spirit. Your flesh gravitates toward what it can see, taste, hear, smell, and feel. Therefore, it leans toward the influence of Satan and his kingdom, which operates in the physical realm. The devil is flesh-oriented, working through carnal, natural things. He tempts you to not believe God by things you can see and feel. On the other hand, the Lord operates in the spirit realm, primarily through His Word. Due to the nature of this intense, continual, inner conflict, you can't just do what you want to do. Either your spirit will dominate you or your flesh will instead!

You cannot please God in your flesh. **"So then they that are in the flesh cannot please God"** (Rom. 8:8). It's not just hard—it's impossible. This means you must identify the flesh and deal with it!

Not "Sinful Nature"

Living after the flesh brings all forms of death. **"Therefore, brethren, we are debtors, not to the flesh, to live after the flesh. For if ye live after the flesh, ye shall die: but if ye through the Spirit do mortify the deeds of the body, ye shall live"** (Rom. 8:12-13). This not only means ultimate physical death (when your spirit and soul separate from your body) but includes everything that leads up to it. **"For the wages of sin is death"** (Rom. 6:23). Biblically speaking, any result of sin is a form of death. Depression, discouragement, anger, bitterness, fear, worry, sickness, poverty, loneliness, etc. are all death. If you live after the flesh, you'll—be sick, impoverished, depressed, angry, etc.—die. Your flesh is Satan's inroad to bring death into your life.

As a born-again believer, your flesh is made up of your soulish and physical realms. However, before you were saved, it also included your fallen human spirit.

My study of the *New International Version* of the Bible (NIV) has shown me that it almost always substitutes the phrase "sinful nature" for what the *King James Version* (KJV) translates "flesh." This interpretation may work to a certain degree, but I've found it misleading in many places. For instance, in Romans, the flesh basically refers to either someone who isn't born again or a born-again believer who isn't living under the control of the Holy Spirit. The phrase "sinful nature" does not accurately convey this truth.

Newness of Life

As Paul taught how God now deals with people based on His grace, not their performance, this raised the question in Romans 6:1. **"What shall we say then? Shall we continue in sin, that grace may abound?"** The answer, of course, is, **"God forbid. How shall we, that are dead to sin, live any longer therein?"** (Rom. 6:2). Your spirit is the part of you that's dead to sin. Your body and soul can still do sinful things, but the born-again part of you cannot.

"Know ye not, that so many of us as were baptized into Jesus Christ were baptized into his death?" (Rom. 6:3). This is talking about being baptized into the body of Christ with the Holy Spirit being the baptizer—not water baptism (1 Cor. 12:13).

There are different baptizers and different elements you're baptized into. After professing faith in Christ, you should follow the Lord and be physically dunked under water as a symbol of what took place at salvation. Also, Jesus will baptize you in the Holy Spirit. But Romans 6:3 is referring to how, when you're born again, you are placed in Christ and He in you. You receive the Spirit of Christ and He receives you. When this baptism took place, you were baptized into His death.

Notice how being baptized into His death is automatic, but walking in newness of life isn't. **"Therefore we are buried with him by baptism into death: that like as Christ was raised up from the dead by the glory of the Father, even so we also should walk in newness of life"** (Rom. 6:4, emphasis mine). Manifesting newness of life is something that should happen.

But it depends on how you renew your mind. **"For if we have been planted together in the likeness of his death, we shall be also in the likeness of his resurrection: Knowing this"** (Rom. 6:5-6). Your spirit died to sin, cannot sin, and has no desire for sin, but this doesn't automatically mean that your soul and body will reflect that change. Your walking in resurrection life depends upon you **"knowing this, that our old man is crucified with him, that the body of sin might be destroyed, that henceforth, we should not serve sin"** (Rom. 6:6).

"Old man" refers to the spirit you had prior to salvation. It's your spirit realm that was dead in trespasses and sins (Eph. 2:1). Your old man no longer exists because it's been crucified, has died, and was buried with Christ. The way some people teach the Scriptures would lead you to believe you have up to four spirits all living somewhere inside you at once (old spirit, new spirit, Spirit of Christ, and Holy Spirit). That's worse than being schizophrenic—it's multiple personalities! God's Word doesn't teach that!

Most Christians today believe they have an old nature and a new nature. That's wrong because your old man died, and your new man is now who you are in the spirit. I'm not going to verify this any further here because my focus is showing you how to overcome the flesh.

Spooked!

The NIV translates "flesh" as your old "sinful nature." That's just too much interpretation! At the new birth, your old nature is crucified, dead, and gone. In its place, God gives you a brand-new spirit, and you become a new creature. That spirit is so united with Christ that there is actually no difference between your born-again spirit and the Spirit of Christ, which was sent into your heart. You literally became one with Him (1 Cor. 6:17). Your born-again spirit is identical to Jesus. The two of you have become one, making a brand-new person. Then, your spirit was sealed, surrounded, and encased by the Holy Spirit!

People embrace this concept of having an old nature that drives them to sin because it logically explains their continued propensity for it. But Romans 6:6 explains what you need to know to be free. Your old man was crucified with Him. Then, the body of sin has to be destroyed!

When you die physically, you leave a body behind. **"For as the body without the spirit is dead, so faith without works is dead also"** (James 2:26). Physical death occurs when your spirit leaves your body. It takes a period of time for your body to begin deteriorating and decaying. Even though your spirit is gone, your physical body can look exactly the same as it did during life for a brief period of time.

Many years ago, my friend worked in the morgue on the 13th floor of Parkland Hospital in Dallas, Texas. One time, he pulled a man out on a slab who was already dead and in there for an autopsy. When my friend turned around to do something, this guy sat up with his mouth open wide and arms dangling at his side. Completely spooked, my friend almost jumped right out the window!

Running down the hall, he dragged somebody in to check this man's vital signs. Dead! After pushing the corpse back down, the medical professional explained, "Sometimes when a person has just died, there will still be electrical impulses in their body. Their muscles contract, and they can sit up like that, but he's not alive." The body still had some of life's mannerisms, but life itself had departed.

One Nature, Two Minds

When you were born again, your old sin nature left behind a body. That's why you still feel a drawing toward sin even though you're dead to it. Your old man was crucified, has died, and now is gone, but its effects are still being felt through your physical body and unrenewed mind.

Your natural mind was programmed to act like the child of the devil that you were before receiving the Lord (Eph. 2:1-2). You were taught how to be selfish, angry, lustful, critical, greedy, bitter, and to do all the other sins that you did. But now that you're born again, your heavenly Father has adopted you into His family and given you a brand-new, righteous nature. However, your old man left behind a body. This means your physical mind will continue functioning like a computer under its prior programming until you renew it to God's Word!

You have one nature but two minds. If you think you have both the old nature and the new one inside, you're going to think you are two different people at once. That's schizophrenic! You only have one nature—the new one. But you do have two different minds—the unrenewed mind (flesh) and the mind of Christ (spirit).

The key is to reprogram your physical mind to agree with your spiritual mind. Your spirit is always for God, always thinks on who you are in Christ, always considers what you have in the Lord, and always believes what you can do in Him. As you renew your natural mind to think like your spirit, you'll experience the life and power of God within you.

Simple, But Not Easy

It's that simple, but not that easy. If you tapped into the spirit realm as a brand-new believer, only listened to who you are in Christ, and let the Holy Spirit instruct you without any negative outside influence (human, religious, or demonic), you would naturally start radiating and manifesting the life of God in your thoughts and actions. However, life's just not that way. You've been programmed wrong and need reprogramming. The enemy lies to you, and friends, family, and religious people say, "Oh no, you don't have the nature of God! You're just an old sinner saved by grace. You can't do these things!" These voices constantly challenge you not to believe what your spirit is saying. Due to this, you manifest the life of God from your spirit only to varying degrees, depending on how well you renew your mind.

Your physical mind decides whether you'll be dominated by your spirit or your flesh. If you don't renew it with God's Word, your natural mind will automatically gravitate toward what it can see, taste, hear, smell, and feel. You must get into God's Word and mix it with faith in order to be led by your spirit. **"Walk in the Spirit, and ye shall not fulfil the lust of the flesh"** (Gal. 5:16).

Buttoning my shirt was a problem for me until I reprogrammed my mind. I'm not sure why, but when I was a kid, I had a hard time buttoning my shirt. Every time I started, I'd get it wrong. When I got down to the bottom, I'd realize I buttoned it incorrectly and had to redo it. Yet today, I have no problem buttoning my shirt. I wear buttoned shirts often and button them correctly the first time without even thinking about it. Buttoning my shirt has become "second nature."

You can mistake something that comes so naturally to you today as your "nature," when in reality, it's something you learned. The reason you still do some of the things you do is because you haven't renewed your mind. Your old sin nature isn't in there forcing you to do things like before you were born again. You've just acted on these negative things and had them reinforced by the carnal world around you so often that they've become established patterns of thinking and acting. If you're born again, you're not evil inside! You just need to reprogram your mind to God's ways of thinking and acting!

Jesus has set you free! There's no sinful nature inside of you that you're warring against. That old man is dead and gone. The only reason you aren't manifesting your freedom in every area of life is because you're ignorant of it. You haven't renewed your mind, and your flesh still dominates you in different ways. Personally, I've experienced a tremendous amount of victory, but I'm still in the process of renewing my mind just like anybody else!

Spirit = spirit

The "flesh" is not really describing a "sinful nature" after you've been born again. Rather, it more accurately refers to every thought, emotion, desire, and part of you that isn't under the control of your brand-new righteous spirit.

110

Technically speaking, what's true of the Holy Spirit is also true of your born-again spirit because they are one. **"But he that is joined unto the Lord is one spirit"** (1 Cor. 6:17). There aren't capital letters in the Greek. Translators decided from the context of a passage whether to render it "Spirit" or "spirit." Either way—Holy Spirit or born-again spirit—the same point is made. **"Walk in the Spirit [spirit], and ye shall not fulfil the lust of the flesh"** (Gal. 5:16, brackets mine).

The thoughts, desires, patterns, and habits that were established in you through the old sinful nature will begin to diminish as you choose to be dominated by your spirit instead. You don't have to continue in bondage to lust, alcohol, hatred, drugs, strife, gossip, depression, sickness, discouragement, disease, poverty, etc. You can break all of those things off because in your spirit, you're already free. It's just a matter of renewing your mind and beginning to see who you are in Christ manifest. As that happens, you won't fulfill the lust of the flesh. Awesome!

Chapter 17

The Impossible Life

"For that which I do I allow not: for what I would, that do I not; but what I hate, that do I. If then I do that which I would not, I consent unto the law that it is good. Now then it is no more I that do it, but sin that dwelleth in me. For I know that in me (<u>that is, in my flesh,</u>) dwelleth no good thing" (Rom. 7:15-18, emphasis mine). Paul knew that the Spirit of Christ indwelt his born-again spirit. Therefore, he couldn't be technically correct and say **"In me...dwelleth no good thing"** without the clarifying statement **"(That is, in my flesh,)."**

Paul acknowledged his born-again spirit, but declared, "There is no good thing in my flesh—my unrenewed mind and physical body, all the external parts of me functioning independent from Christ. There's nothing good about that! I'm going to have to lay this flesh down and receive a new body and a new soul, which are completely renewed and think exactly like God."

"For I know that in me (that is, in my flesh,) dwelleth no good thing: for to will is present with me; but how to perform that which is good I find not. For the good that I would I do not: but the evil which I would not, that I do. Now if I do that I would not, it is no more I that do it, but sin that dwelleth in me. I find then a law, that, when I would do good, evil is present with me. For I delight in the law of God after the inward man: But I see another law in my members, warring against the law of my mind, and bringing me into captivity to the law of sin which is in my members" (Rom. 7:18-23).

Sounds a lot like what he wrote in Galatians 5:17, "For the flesh lusteth against the Spirit, and the Spirit against the flesh: and these are contrary the one to the other: so that ye cannot do the things that ye would." Romans 7:24 summarizes Paul's dismal dilemma, "O wretched man that I am! who shall deliver me from the body of this death?"

My associate, Don Krow, has an excellent message from this passage entitled "USDA Choice Flesh." He goes into much more detail than I will here. Don preached it at a Ministers' Conference and literally changed people's entire attitude toward what these scriptures are really communicating. I encourage you to get ahold of it!

Without Supernatural Assistance

Romans 7 doesn't teach that Paul was constantly trying and failing to do the right thing. He wasn't describing his present Christian life and saying that this is the way that it is. Paul wasn't confessing that after all those years, he was still struggling with lust, sexual sin, anger, and bitterness. Neither was he saying, "You have this flesh, and try as you might, but you can never beat it."

Paul was simply describing the inability of the flesh—your physical ability, natural mind, emotions, and actions all independent from Christ—to please God. You cannot overcome your flesh on your own; you have to start living from who you are in Christ. Your spirit man is completely changed and infused with the life of God. You can only please Him through living by your spirit!

The Christian life isn't just difficult to live—it's impossible! In your flesh, you can't do what the Lord has told you to do. He's commanded you to just bear it when someone insults you. If they slap you on the face, you're to turn the other cheek. If they sue you and take away your coat, you're to give them your cloak as well. If someone forces you to carry their burden one mile against your will, go two miles (Matt. 5:39-41). Your natural self, independent of God, just won't do things like that!

It's natural to be self-serving, self-seeking, and self-promoting! If somebody slaps you on the cheek, you want to hit both of theirs. If someone takes something from you through a lawsuit, you want to hire the best lawyer to sue them back. But the Lord's told you, "Do the opposite." Without supernatural assistance, it's impossible to do what Jesus commands! That's why Paul declared, "It's no longer me that lives but Christ who lives through me" (Gal. 2:20).

490

There's a tremendous amount of liberty that comes with recognizing and releasing Christ in you. You don't have to say in the flesh "Well, I will to love you" and turn the other cheek through gritted teeth. It's much better to pray, "Father, in myself, I'd like to knock their block off. My flesh cannot do this," (Paul described this in Romans 7), "but in my spirit, I can do all things through Christ who strengthens me. I have the same spirit that Jesus had when He hung on the cross and forgave the very people who crucified Him." (You've read that in God's Word and believed it.) "Father, I don't feel like it right now, but I know my spirit is the same one that enabled Jesus to extend mercy to those who mocked Him. In the natural, I can't do this. Father, please live through me now. Give me a supernatural compassion for this person so I can love them!"

Peter thought he was being very generous when he asked, "How many times should I forgive my brother—up to seven times a day?" Jesus answered, "Not seven times but seventy times seven!" That's 490 times in one day! This was His way of communicating that there shouldn't be a limit on your forgiveness (Matt. 18:21-22).

The Lord wants you to forgive totally—as much and as many times as it takes! In your flesh, you might be able to forgive a person for some minor things once, twice, or even seven times in a day (Peter thought he might be able to do that). But what Jesus asked goes far beyond your human ability. The only way you can forgive like that is by saying, "Father, I can't do it, but You can. Lord, please love them through me." When you humble yourself, turning away from your own natural ability and to God and His divine ability, you'll discover a supernatural strength flowing through you!

You have an unlimited supply of God's kind of love in your spirit. **"Charity suffereth long, and is kind; charity envieth not; charity vaunteth not itself, is not puffed up, Doth not behave itself unseemly, seeketh not her own, is not easily provoked, thinketh no evil; Rejoiceth not in iniquity, but rejoiceth in the truth; Beareth all things, believeth all things, hopeth all things, endureth all things"** (1 Cor. 13:4-7). His love never fails (verse 8)!

In your spirit, you have an unlimited ability to forgive, en-dure, believe, and hope! If you catch yourself remarking "I can't put up with this person any more. I just can't take it. I'm at the end of my rope!" what you're really saying is, "I've come to the end of my flesh!" That's good! Now let your spirit take over!

You Can Too!

Pray, *"God,* I'm sorry! I've been trying this in myself, which is why I'm burned out, frustrated, and angry. Forgive me and live Your life through me. I believe Your Word. In the spirit, I am a brand-new person. If I would walk in the spirit, I won't fulfill the lust of the flesh." (Then, start meditating on who you are and what you have in Christ.) "By faith, this is who I choose to believe I am."

That's renewing your mind and releasing the supernatural life of God out of your spirit into your soul and body. When your physical mind comes into agreement with your spiritual mind, you can literally begin to hope, endure, and believe in things that you couldn't have done by your natural self!

I've been able to love the many different people who have come out against me. A guy I was witnessing to spat in my face. People have tried to physically assault me. Some other well-known ministers publicly called me a "cult leader" and "of the devil." A guy stole $20,000 from our ministry. I've even been kidnapped and had threats on my life! But in all of this (and more), I can truthfully tell you that I have nothing against any of these people. I harbor no evil thoughts and never spend any time even thinking about them. I've completely forgiven each and every one. How? I renewed my mind to God's Word and released the love and forgiveness that's in my spirit. You can do it too!

Releasing Your True Identity

You can't please God if you're in the flesh! Romans 7 describes living by your own natural, carnal ability. That's why the results are defeat, failure, and an inability to do the desired good (Rom. 7:19). In your flesh, you can't overcome, turn the other cheek, or forgive an unlimited number of times. That's why Paul said of his flesh, **"O wretched man that I am! who shall deliver me from the body of this death?"** (Rom. 7:24). In other words, Paul asked, "Who will deliver me from this flesh?"

The very next verse contains the answer! **"I thank God through Jesus Christ our Lord"** (Rom. 7:25). Deliverance from the flesh comes through living by who you are in the spirit! From here, Paul launches right into Romans 8 with **"There is therefore."** **"Therefore"** refers back to what has previously been said, which is that the flesh cannot please God (Rom. 7). Therefore, you must walk after the Spirit (Rom. 8).

"There is therefore now no condemnation to them which are in Christ Jesus, who walk not after the flesh, but after the Spirit" (Rom. 8:1). Your spirit is the only part of you in Christ Jesus. If you are in the spirit, there is no condemnation to you whatsoever. That's good news!

Romans 8 is one of the most victorious chapters in the whole Bible! Why? It's written from the perspective of your born-again spirit. The frustration of living after the flesh described in Romans 7 is not the typical Christian life. Romans 7 speaks of a person trying to please God through their own natural effort. "O God, I'm trying to do better. I want to do better, but I just can't!" Why? It's impossible to serve God in the flesh. The word "spirit" is only used once in Romans 7. In contrast, it's used 21 times in Romans 8. It's Romans 8 that describes the typical Christian life. You've got to get over into the spirit!

This revelation of spirit, soul, and body unlocks so much of the Christian life! How can you live in the spirit if you don't know that it was your spirit that changed? When you understand that, you can begin comprehending that who you are and what you have in Christ doesn't fluctuate based on your performance. How can you release something you don't know or don't believe you have? Once you do believe, you must reject the flesh and walk by who you are in the spirit. Cultivate a good image of who you are in Christ, and let that become the real you. It's just a matter of discovering and releasing your true identity!

An Extroverted Introvert

Through this, God's done a miracle in my life! I was extremely introverted before being turned on to the Lord. Because of nervousness and self-consciousness, I couldn't look someone in the face and talk without stammering. Now, God has me speaking to millions of people daily through television and radio. I've ministered to people face to face in meetings all around the world, sometimes up to five thousand at once. Yet, I'm not afraid because it doesn't bother me anymore. I'm focused on who I am in the spirit!

My flesh is the same as it always was. I still have a tendency to be introverted. In fact, when I'm not focused on the Lord and someone catches me in the flesh, I still want to withdraw, not exert myself, and just go sit in the background. This natural part of me hasn't changed.

Most people think they're improving their flesh when they're born again. That's simply not true! You don't improve your natural self through the Christian life, you just become better at denying it. The improvement comes by choosing to recognize your new identity in Christ and letting those thoughts and actions manifest from your spirit.

When I take personality tests now, I always score the maximum in every category for extroverts. That's who I've chosen to be and who I've become in Christ. It's who my born-again spirit is. If you could somehow test me apart from my godly reactions, you'd find I'm still an introvert in my flesh.

Living from the Spirit

The Christian life isn't your natural flesh becoming stronger in godliness so that you don't need the Holy Spirit as much as when you first began. Rather, it's growing stronger in the spirit and weaker in the flesh. The flesh's dominance steadily diminishes as you learn to consistently depend on and draw out more of what's in your spirit.

Focus on who you are in the spirit by meditating on God's Word, and your flesh will bow the knee to the spirit's rule and reign. **"Walk in the Spirit, and ye shall not fulfil the lust of the flesh. For the flesh lusteth against the Spirit, and the Spirit against the flesh: and these are contrary the one to the other: so that ye cannot do the things that ye would"** (Gal. 5:16-17). You'll break the control of the flesh as you base your identity and potential on what the Word says about who you are in Christ. Instead of being controlled by your old carnal self, your spirit man will begin to dominate.

My flesh is still basically timid and shy, but my spirit is as bold as a lion (Prov. 28:1)! Some people who travel on airlines push their way up to the counter and make demands whenever something goes wrong. I'm quite the opposite. I actually set my travel agent cards aside because the ticket agents almost never grant me any of those discounts. I'm just not a pushy guy! Yet, I can be very bold and assertive when it comes to spiritual matters, or anything else of value to me. People have challenged me in services before. It's like the spirit of might comes upon me, and I just take care of it (Is. 11:2). That's because I've learned how to live more from my spirit than my flesh.

Chapter 18

Mind Your Spirit

Through spiritual dyslexia, most people perceive Galatians 5:16 completely backwards! **"This I say then, Walk in the Spirit, and ye shall not fulfil the lust of the flesh."** They recognize that the flesh and the spirit are contrary but assume that they're automatically walking in the spirit if they just deny their flesh. Therefore, they put all of their focus on quitting this and rejecting that, thinking, *If I can just stop doing these bad things and having these foul thoughts, then I'll be in the spirit!* Wrong! This verse doesn't say "Walk in the flesh, and you'll hinder the spirit" or "Overcome the flesh, and then you'll walk in the spirit." No, it declares just the opposite: "Walk in the spirit, and you won't fulfill the lust of the flesh!"

Darkness is simply the absence of light. You can't get rid of darkness by shoveling it out of the room. However, if you turn on a light, it'll flee! When you walk in the spirit (turn on the light), by default—as a byproduct—you won't fulfill the lust of the flesh (darkness flees). Willpower is the shovel of the flesh. If you feel

121

you can't really accept who you are in Christ until after you overcome the darkness in your life—drinking, cussing, smoking, or whatever problems you currently have—you'll just end up frustrated and stuck (Rom. 7). It's not that God won't release His power to you; it's just that you haven't yet flipped the switch! Lay that shovel down and turn on the light! Get into God's Word, and start recognizing and meditating on who you are in Christ. As you focus your attention continually on the reality of your new identity, the brightness of who you are in the spirit will begin to shine in and through you to such a degree that it'll break the control of the flesh and deliver you from these external problems. Light always overwhelms and chases away the dark!

A friend of mine used to be a well-known secular entertainer who wrote several famous songs. While in this profession, he became born again. After finishing a concert at midnight, he'd hop on the bus with his musicians and start traveling to their next gig. Excited about God and His Word, my friend actually snorted cocaine off the pages of His Bible so he could stay awake and keep reading about how much the Lord loved him!

Today, this man has been a pastor for over twenty years! How did he overcome his flesh and its bad habits? Did he quit snorting cocaine and all the other ungodly things he was doing first? No! This man didn't let his vices keep him from beginning to find out what God's Word said about him. He centered his attention on discovering who he was in Christ and what all Jesus had done for him. As those things became reality to him, he finally came to a place where God led him out of that lifestyle.

God wants you to come to Him just as you are! After you're born again and changed inside, renew your mind to who you are in Christ. As you find out who you are in your spirit, you'll change outwardly as a result. If you'll just start walking in the spirit by focusing your attention on the things of God, regardless of what your flesh is like, you'll break its dominion over you!

Focus: Quality & Quantity

You can know whether you're walking in the spirit or not by what your attention is on. **"For they that are after the flesh do mind the things of the flesh; but they that are after the Spirit the things of the Spirit"** (Rom. 8:5). What you're thinking about will tell you whether you're in the flesh or in the spirit!

Where is your focus? If the doctor says you're going to die, are you more dominated by his word or God's Word? Are you imagining and anticipating sickness, disease, and death? Or are you focused on the scriptures that declare He's taken away all your sickness and by His stripes you were healed of every disease? Are you centered in on the spirit or the flesh?

If your mind is stayed on the things of the flesh, then you're in the flesh. You cannot please God, nor will you be able to succeed against this ailment. You'll die physically even though God's healing and raising-from-the-dead power is already inside your born-again spirit. Whatever your mind focuses on determines whether you're in the flesh or not. It's really that simple!

By learning to keep your mind stayed on God, your spirit will dominate and control your flesh. **"For to be carnally minded is death; but to be spiritually minded is life and peace"** (Rom. 8:6). This isn't just quality time; it's both quality *and* quantity of time spent focused on the things of God.

Fleshly mindedness is death. "Carnal" literally means "of the five senses." Carnal mindedness is being fleshly, physical, and outward minded instead of spiritually minded. It's being dominated by your five senses. If your body is facing sickness and you're more in tune with and sensitive to what you feel (flesh) than what you believe (Word), then you're carnal. To be carnally minded is death, but to be spiritually minded is life and peace.

Whose Report Will You Believe?

You need to get to where you believe God's report more than the world's! You've crossed over into the spirit when God's Word dominates you more than what you can see, taste, hear, smell, and feel. Instead of letting the devil tell you what you can't do or somebody else saying that you'll die or your checkbook telling you you're in deep trouble again, you focus your attention on what God says about you, what He says you have, and what He says you can do. Once you do that, you'll find it'll break the dominion, the power, and the control of the flesh over you.

Physical healing was purchased through Christ's atonement. It's not just a "P.S." to forgiveness of sin; healing is an integral part of what Jesus died to produce. In fact, His sacrifice provides physical healing just as much as forgiveness of sin. God would no more give someone sickness than lead them into sin. Why? Jesus shed His precious blood to completely redeem us from both! (For an in-depth look at healing, I recommend my teaching entitled *God Wants You Well.*)

Seeing a truth doesn't mean you'll automatically profit from it. Actually, conflict will normally arise! Hebrews 10:32 reveals that once you're enlightened, you endure **"a great fight of afflictions."** Why? Satan immediately comes to steal the Word before it takes root in your heart and produces (Mark 4:15,19). He attempts to dislodge it when you're at your youngest, when a truth is still new to you, before it's rooted and established as part of who you are.

Once I saw in the Word that it's always God's will to heal, the fight was on! Satan came against me, and I started experiencing sickness more than ever before. Immediately, there was intense conflict between my flesh and spirit. The spirit declared, "By His stripes I was healed (1 Pet. 2:24); it's already done (Eph. 1:18)" and "The same power that raised Jesus Christ from the dead is inside of me (Eph. 1:19-20)." In my spirit, I had this resurrection power, but my flesh kept arguing, "You're sick! You feel terrible and you're about to throw up. Admit it!" There was this incredible conflict between what I saw in my spirit through God's Word and what I felt in my physical body. My flesh and my spirit were fighting each other!

This was just my unrenewed mind, not some old nature inside trying to make me disbelieve God. For a number of years, my old man taught me how to believe only what I could see, taste, hear, smell, and feel. Anything and everything else was stupid! When he was crucified, my mind was left behind, programmed to sense knowledge. Everything in my physical, natural, fleshly realm screamed, "You're sick!" My body told me that I hurt. Other people commented on how bad I looked. Therefore, it was a real struggle for my mind to believe what I couldn't see!

I just determined in my heart that I would not give up or give in until I saw with my physical eyes the truth of God's Word manifest in my body. I was so committed to the fact that what God said about me was true that I decided to make myself believe it.

Cracking the Dam

At the time, I was living and pastoring a small church in Segoville, Texas. I preached healing and had revelation knowledge of it, but I was sick in my body. The devil was fighting me. My flesh and my spirit were butting heads!

Since faith without works is dead, I decided one night not to just lay in bed and act sick (James 2:17, 20, 26). I didn't want to kill my faith by giving in to the pressure. However, it was physically impossible for me to stand up because I was so ill. I had to kneel on the floor in the living room so Jamie could go ahead and sleep. Putting my Bible on the wood floor in front of me, I determined in my heart that I was going to fight this thing!

I spent hours just quoting scriptures on healing. I didn't stop because I knew I'd fall asleep out of sheer exhaustion if I did. I'd confess aloud, "By His stripes, I was healed." My body would counter, "Oh no, you're not!" Then I'd answer, "Yes, I am—the Word says so!" This fight continued several hours while I pushed my Bible along and crawled around the room on hands and knees just to stay awake.

You don't have to do it the way I did, but you will have to overcome the same conflict! You don't just say, "All right, I see the truth. Flesh, I now renounce you and choose to walk by the spirit!" No, it'll be a traumatic experience when you turn around and head the other direction. Your mind and emotions have been indulged now for many years. They've always said that whatever you see is more real than what's invisible. There's going to be a fight, and it probably won't all happen in just one evening's time!

That night proved to be a major break for me. I cracked the dam of flesh that held back the flow of God's life in me. My spirit began dominating from that point forward little by little. I'm still dealing with these same things, but I've grown a lot. I'm seeing tremendous victory in my life, and I'm able to help many other people. I'm still in process, but I'm renewing my mind and winning the battle between my flesh and my spirit.

The Test

Recently, I was required to take a treadmill test while receiving a qualifying physical for an insurance policy. However, since I refused to allow them to shave my chest hair, the electrodes fell off after only twelve minutes. Several weeks later, the insurance company called and said they couldn't insure me. They cited the fact that my readings indicated I had a serious heart problem that surfaced at about the twelfth minute of the test. When I asked them if the electrodes falling off would've made a difference or not, they decided to give me another test.

This time I let them shave my chest, but not before informing the nurse that she was removing virgin hair! I finished the test without incident and waited for the doctor to review my results. He was fine with my readings up until about the thirteenth minute of the test. That's when he got a worried look on his face and told me I had a serious problem. This medical professional then advised me of my "need" to see a specialist that very day and began writing out the note for me to give to this other doctor.

I boldly looked this man in the face and declared, "I don't believe your results!" It was easy to see that he wasn't used to someone countering his opinion. However, I challenged him to look again at the printout and then honestly tell me that I had a heart problem.

He replied, "Well, this doesn't really say you have a heart problem. It's just that your results are completely typical. Since everyone's heart is a little different, you could be totally healthy. I just think you should go get another test!"

"That's not what you said!" I thundered. "You told me I had a serious heart problem, not that there's a small chance and you think I should get another opinion."

This guy backed down and sputtered, "You're fine… just forget about that other test."

Most people would have taken the word of this doctor over the Word of God, which emphatically declares that we're healed. By the time they finished obsessing about it, their hearts would have failed—from fear (Luke 21:26)! The next time you're faced with a report that's contrary to God's, who will you choose to believe?

Overcome Your Flesh

You overcome by being mindful of what God's Word says about you—especially the New Testament. When you're Word minded, you're spiritually minded because God's words are spirit and life (John 6:63). In your spirit, you're completely changed, eternal, sanctified, holy, and perfected forever. As Jesus is—so are you! If you'd dominate yourself with those thoughts, all it would produce is life and peace.

If you're having something other than life and peace, then you're something other than spiritually minded (Rom. 8:6). You may desire the right things, praying and begging God for them, but you don't receive victory by desiring or begging for it. You receive the victory He's already achieved and provided for you by focusing your attention on the spirit. When you do that, you'll overcome.

In my opinion, you won't manifest much of the life of God if you're plugged into the world through radio, television, newspapers, and magazines. It takes a lot of effort—real effort—to keep your focus on the things of God. How can you expect different results when you read, watch, listen to, and think all the same things as your unbelieving neighbors? That's ignorance gone to seed! Sure, you might be able to add a devotion and intellectually know that God wants you healed, prospered, and delivered from oppression. You may even have a desire for and a sensitivity to God that they don't have. But as far as results go, you won't really experience any more of God's miraculous power in your life as long as you continue thinking on the same carnal things that they do pretty much all day long. To get different results, you have to do something differently!

If you mind the things of the flesh, then you'll be after the flesh; the physical realm will dominate you. You won't be able to please God (Rom. 8:8) or experience the victory that's available to you. In order to release God's power and life, you must overcome the flesh by continually focusing your mind on who you are and what you have in the spirit.

Chapter 19

Time to Leave!

When you make Jesus Christ Lord of your life by truly believing on Him, an instantaneous change takes place. This change
occurs in your spirit, not your flesh—body or soul. Whether the
change ever manifests itself in your physical realm depends on
what you think.

The flesh, your natural self, pulls in one direction, and your
spirit leads you in another. How you think determines what you
experience. If your mind stays only on physical things—not even
necessarily sinful things, just physical—then you'll be limited to
and dominated by your flesh. You might even be a very moral
person, but you won't experience the supernatural life of God.

The only way you'll experience the power of God within
you is to walk in the spirit. Believing to raise someone from the
dead goes beyond just living a good life. You must believe in
something that has no proof or evidence in the physical realm
whatsoever. You have to get beyond the physical and acknowl-

edge that there is a spiritual world. As you recognize your true power and believe, the spiritual realm will become more real to you than the physical.

This applies to prosperity too! There will be times when there's no basis for faith in your physical facts. Your bank statement won't prove it. Everything in the natural may be coming against the Word, but if you stay in the spirit, fixed on what His Word says, you'll be able to see yourself prosperous when everyone else tries to repossess your house, car, etc. As you hold on to God's Word, your spirit will overcome your flesh and break its dominion. That's when you'll see the Word manifest!

Peace

You can be spiritually minded! Whatever you continually think on will dominate you (Prov. 23:7). If it's who you are and what you have in Christ, then that's what will eventually manifest itself in your physical life.

One-third of your salvation is already complete! Your born-again spirit isn't in the process of growing or maturing. Right now in your spirit, you are exactly the way you'll be throughout eternity (1 John 4:17). You have a physical body and soul that haven't been changed yet. They are subject to change and can change, but it's not automatic. However, the change of your spirit at salvation was total, complete, and automatic.

Whether you ever see your true spiritual potential released into your physical life or not depends on what you think (Rom. 12:2). If natural things—either sinful or just plain carnal—dominate and control your thoughts, you'll shut off the flow of God's Spirit through you. But if you dominate yourself with the truths of His Word and get beyond the natural limitations of your five senses, you can start releasing the supernatural life that's inside you.

You'll be able to experience a peace that passes understanding. Even when it seems like everyone's against you and everything's crashing in the physical realm, you'll enjoy God's supernatural peace as long as you stay focused on the Word. **"And the peace of God, which passeth all understanding, shall keep your hearts and minds through Christ Jesus"** (Phil. 4:7).

On the night before His crucifixion, Jesus told His disciples, **"Let not your heart be troubled: ye believe in God, believe also in me"** (John 14:1). To the natural mind, this sounds unreasonable in light of the situation. Their Messiah, the One they loved and worshiped, was about to be executed. There's no natural way they could have peace in the midst of something like that, but Jesus had given them His Word. He'd told them many times, "I'll be crucified, but I'll rise again on the third day." If they had meditated on and dominated themselves by what Jesus had said, they would have released the supernatural peace of God they needed for that trying situation. (Christ's last minute instructions to His disciples for overcoming crisis situations are thoroughly unpacked in my teaching entitled *Christian Survival Kit.*)

What Will You Think?

If you want to experience God's best, you must understand these truths concerning spirit, soul, and body. You have unlimited potential, but it's all in the spirit. The victory God's given you isn't in your flesh, it's in the part of you that's been born again. As you mature in the Christian life, you don't become less carnal; you just let less carnality dominate and manifest because you're yielded to the spirit instead.

Through God's Word, concentrate on seeing who you are in Christ. Spend less time feeding the flesh and focus on the spirit instead. Surround yourself with people who speak faith, are positive, and center in on the potential we have in Christ instead of those who gripe and complain. You'll develop an entire mentality based on your new identity in Christ as you dominate yourself with what you see in the spiritual mirror of God's Word.

Nothing can separate you from God's love because your born-again spirit has been sanctified and perfected forever. God is a Spirit, and He sees you in the spirit (John 4:24). He fellowships with you Spirit to born-again spirit. God doesn't give you what you deserve based on your thoughts and physical actions in your flesh; rather, He deals with you in the spirit realm. That's why He'll receive you at any time, in any condition—you're His beloved child!

You're constantly being fed information and drawn in one of two directions—the flesh or the spirit (Gal. 5:17). The Holy Spirit always endeavors to draw you toward God and remind you of your new identity in Christ. Satan, through the world, its images and voices—news media, movies, books, newspapers, magazines, associations, and even church organizations who are mistaken in some of their beliefs—constantly pushes you to accept defeat. What you continually think on is what you'll experience (Prov. 23:7).

Your flesh and spirit constantly fight each other in your mind. God proclaims, "You can do all things through Christ." The world answers, "No, you can't. You're just a failure!" On and on, the daily battle rages. That's why this life-changing truth isn't just something you learn one time and conclude, "I've got it!" This understanding of spirit, soul, and body should motivate you to aggressively pursue renewing your mind to God's Word—a process that'll continue for the rest of your life!

Soak Your Mind

Soak your mind in these truths that God has spoken. You might need to go back and reread this book in a week or in a couple of months. Perhaps you should consider ordering the audio series so you can listen to this teaching again and again. Whatever you do, meditate these truths until they come alive to you. Then, keep them refreshed by occasionally coming back to them.

God spoke these truths to me over 35 years ago, but I'm still in the process of renewing my mind to them. Over time, He's been expanding, developing, and giving me even more understanding on this. I feel like the Apostle Paul, who after twenty or more years of knowing and serving God, said, **"Brethren, I count not myself to have apprehended: but this one thing I do, forgetting those things which are behind, and reaching forth unto those things which are before, I press toward the mark for the prize of the high calling of God in Christ Jesus"** (Phil. 3:13-14).

Don't be discouraged! I'm not saying you have to wait a long time before you see any results. I just want you to know that until you see Him face to face, you never arrive, you just leave. And if the Lord has spoken to you through this teaching, you need to leave right now! Turn from carnal mindedness, and start being dominated by your born-again spirit instead. Discover the realities concerning who you are in the spirit, and let them control you. When you do, you'll experience life and peace. It really is that simple!

But it's not easy! In fact, changing your focus from the flesh to the spirit is one of the hardest things you'll ever do. It's a gradual, but total, reprogramming of your natural mind to agree with your spirit. Through renewing your mind to God's Word, you can become spiritually minded!

What God has spoken to you through this book has the potential of radically changing your life, but applying these truths will take some real focus and effort on your part. However, the good news is that God wants you to fully understand and walk in them even more than you do! He'll faithfully do His part if you'll just head in that direction acknowledging that "God, it's going to

135

take a miracle to renew my mind! It's so used to being dominated by the flesh. I'm really going to need Your help!" The Holy Spirit will reveal to you who you are in Christ. He'll show you Jesus, spiritual truth, and reality. It just takes commitment and effort on your part to focus on the Word and the spirit.

Begin Now

In light of what you've read, I encourage you to pray out loud the following prayer from your heart:

Father, I open my heart to the Holy Spirit to continue revealing these truths to me. I recognize that this is a process and not just a one-time thing. Therefore, I ask You to give me greater revelation of spirit, soul, and body throughout the rest of my life. As I apply what You've shown me, please encourage me with some quick results. I want to establish new patterns of walking by the spirit so I can live a full and effective life in You.

Thank You for bringing these truths to my remembrance when I need them. Thank You for helping me to share them with others so they too can break free from their flesh's dominion. Thank You for setting me free and using me to set many others free too! I love You, Father! Amen.

Receiving Jesus as your Savior

Choosing to receive Jesus Christ as your Lord and Savior is the most important decision you'll ever make!

God's Word promises, **"That if thou shalt confess with thy mouth the Lord Jesus, and shalt believe in thine heart that God hath raised him from the dead, thou shalt be saved. For with the heart man believeth unto righteousness; and with the mouth confession is made unto salvation"** (Rom. 10:9-10). **"For whosoever shall call upon the name of the Lord shall be saved"** (Rom. 10:13).

By His grace, God has already done everything to provide salvation. Your part is simply to believe and receive.

Pray out loud, *"Jesus, I confess that You are my Lord and Savior. I believe in my heart that God raised You from the dead. By faith in Your Word, I receive salvation now. Thank You for saving me!"*

The very moment you commit your life to Jesus Christ, the truth of His Word instantly comes to pass in your spirit. Now that you're born again, there's a brand-new you!

Receiving the Holy Spirit

As His child, your loving heavenly Father wants to give you the supernatural power you need to live this new life.

"For every one that asketh receiveth; and he that seeketh findeth; and to him that knocketh it shall be opened...how much more shall your heavenly Father give the Holy Spirit to them that ask him?" (Luke 11:10-13).

All you have to do is ask, believe, and receive!

Pray, *"Father, I recognize my need for Your power to live this new life. Please fill me with Your Holy Spirit. By faith, I receive it right now! Thank You for baptizing me! Holy Spirit, You are welcome in my life!"*

Congratulations—now you're filled with God's supernatural power!

Some syllables from a language you don't recognize will rise up from your heart to your mouth (1 Cor. 14:14). As you speak them out loud by faith, you're releasing God's power from within and building yourself up in the spirit (1 Cor. 14:4). You can do this whenever and wherever you like!

It doesn't really matter whether you felt anything or not when you prayed to receive the Lord and His Spirit. If you believed in your heart that you received, then God's Word promises you did. **"Therefore I say unto you, What things soever ye desire, when ye pray, believe that ye receive them, and ye shall have them"** (Mark 11:24). God always honors His Word—believe it!

Please contact me and let me know that you've prayed to receive Jesus as your Savior or be filled with the Holy Spirit. I would like to rejoice with you and help you understand more fully what has taken place in your life. I'll send you a free gift that will help you understand and grow in your new relationship with the Lord. *"Welcome to your new life!"*

Recomended Materials

Whose Righteousness?

What is righteousness? What makes a person righteous? Is it even possible to obtain righteousness? In this series, discover the answers to these questions and more. Every Christian's relationship with God is based on their understanding of righteousness.

Item Code: 1022   3-Tape album
Item Code: 1022-C   3-CD album

The Gospel: The Power Of God

The book of Romans is Paul's greatest masterpiece on the doctrine of grace. Nowhere else in Scripture is the mystery of God's grace revealed more thoroughly or more simply. This series helps the listener discover the book of Romans' liberating truths, which have literally changed the world.

Item Code: 1014   4-Tape album
Item Code: 1014-C   4-CD album

Paul's Letter To The Galatians

The Apostle Paul was ruthless in dealing with religious legalism and so is Andrew. This album is a verse-by-verse study of the book of Galatians. Here, Paul presents the same great truths of grace that were so masterfully explicated in the book of Romans, but in this letter, Paul uses a hard-hitting approach to remove deception. Teaching from Galatians, Andrew answers the age-old question once and for all: What role does performance play in our relationship with God?

Item Code: 1016   6-Tape album
Item Code: 1016-C   6-CD album

The True Nature Of God

Are you confused about the nature of God? Is He the God of judgment found in the Old Testament or the God of mercy and grace found in the New Testament? Andrew's revelation on this subject will set you free and give you a confidence in your relationship with God like never before. This is truly nearly-too-good-to-be-true news.

Item Code: 1002   3-Tape album
Item Code: 1002-C   3-CD album

Positive Ministry Of The Holy Spirit

When you blow it and you're feeling guilty, is it the Holy Spirit convicting you, or is your conscience condemning you? How do you differentiate the two? In this series, Andrew reveals the key from God's Word. You don't want to miss this!

Item Code: 1020   3-Tape album
Item Code: 1020-C   3-CD album

God's Kind Of Love: The Cure For What Ails Ya!

Symptoms: 1. Tired of trying to love people
               2. Feel unappreciated by others
               3. Believe God only blesses when you're good
               4. Find yourself asking "Why God?" when faced
                  with problems

Diagnosis: Spiritual dyslexia—highly contagious, can be fatal if not treated

Cure: God's kind of love

Prescription: Daily dose of the album *God's Kind of Love: The Cure for What Ails Ya!* until symptoms disappear.

Item Code: 1015   3-Tape album
Item Code: 1015-C   3-CD album

About the Author

Andrew Wommack

For over three decades Andrew has traveled America and the world teaching the truth of the Gospel. His profound revelation of the Word of God is taught with clarity and simplicity, emphasizing God's unconditional love and the balance between grace and faith. He reaches millions of people through the daily *Gospel Truth* radio and television programs, broadcast both domestically and internationally. He founded Charis Bible College in 1994 and has since established CBC extension colleges in other major cities of America and around the world. Andrew has produced a library of teaching materials, available in print, audio, and visual formats. And, as it has been from the beginning, his ministry continues to distribute free audio tapes and CDs to those who cannot afford them.

Contact Information

Andrew Wommack Ministries
P.O. Box 3333
Colorado Springs, CO 80934
Helpline Phone: 719-635-1111
website: www.awmi.net

Andrew Wommack Ministries of Europe
P.O. Box 4392
Walsall WS1 9AR
England
Helpline Phone: +44 (0) 1922 473 300
website: www.awme.net